THE
SUPERMAN
SYNDROME

THE SUPERMAN SYNDROME

Finding God's Strength
Where You Least Expect It

JACK KUHATSCHEK

ZondervanPublishingHouse
Grand Rapids, Michigan

A Division of HarperCollinsPublishers

The Superman Syndrome
Copyright © 1995 by Jack Kuhatschek

Requests for information should be addressed to:

ZondervanPublishingHouse
Grand Rapids, Michigan 49530

Library of Congress Cataloging-in-Publication Data

Kuhatschek, Jack, 1949–
    The superman syndrome: finding God's strength where you least expect it /
Jack Kuhatschek.
      p. cm.
    ISBN: 0-310-49771-X (alk. paper)
      1. Christian life. 2. Power (Christian theology). 3. Kuhatschek, Jack, 1949– .
I. Title.
    BV4501.2.K765   1995
    248.4—dc20
                                         95-23199
                                             CIP

This edition printed on acid-free paper and meets the American National Standards
Institute Z39.48 standard.

Edited by Sandy Vander Zicht and Robin Schmitt
Interior design by Sherri L. Hoffman

Printed in the United States of America

95 96 97 98 99 00 01 02 /❖ DH/ 10 9 8 7 6 5 4 3 2 1

To my mother and father,
Mary Adelaide and Bill Kuhatschek,
who recently celebrated their golden anniversary
and who have been a source of strength for me
throughout my life

CONTENTS

THE SUPERMAN SYNDROME

THE UNEXPECTED GUEST

I was ready to quit. I had only been a Christian for a few weeks, but I felt confused and frustrated, and God didn't seem to be holding up his end of the bargain. Where was he? Why had he abandoned me, when I longed to feel his presence and power in my life? As I went upstairs to bed I had no idea of the overwhelming experience I would have later that evening.

I had become a Christian on November 8, 1966, at the Billy Graham movie *The Restless Ones*. I almost didn't make it to the movie.

Our Young Life club planned to meet at our normal location and then drive to the theater in north Dallas. I called a friend named David who had always gone with me to Young Life. "I just don't feel like going tonight," he said, "but you can always go by yourself."

By myself, I thought as I hung up the phone. *I don't want to go by myself.* I was shy, and the prospect of going alone made me feel uncomfortable. But my desire to go was stronger than my hesitation, so reluctantly I got into the car and drove to the meeting.

When I arrived, our Young Life leader said that everyone with a car should bring it near the entrance so that those without cars could get a ride to the theater. As I pulled my Pontiac convertible up to the door, people began streaming out of the building and getting into everyone's car but mine. They were walking in front of my car, behind it, around it—everywhere but in it. When the last person came out of the building, I was still sitting there alone, feeling exposed and embarrassed.

Again I was faced with a choice. I was strongly tempted to "save face" by driving out of the parking lot and heading home. But for some reason, I knew I needed to go to the movie. At the last minute I swallowed my pride, parked my car, and asked another driver (whose car was *full* of people) if I could ride with him.

Once inside the theater, I watched the movie and discovered that Billy Graham wasn't a politician, as I had thought, but an evangelist! (I had not been raised in a Christian home.) I don't remember much about the film, but at the end, in typical Billy Graham fashion, someone went to the front of the theater and asked all those who wanted to receive Christ as their Savior and Lord to come forward.

I expected everyone to get up and go forward with me. After all, this was a religious group, and I assumed that they wanted to show their support for Jesus Christ. But not one person in my row—including the Young Life leader—got up. I was in the middle of the row, and I didn't want to go forward by myself, so I was tempted to stay in my seat. But something told me that if I didn't get up, I might not ever have this chance again. As I sat there the inner urgings of the Holy Spirit grew stronger than my resistance. Finally I rose from my seat and eased my way past all the people who were between me and the aisle. Stepping over spilled popcorn and discarded candy wrappers, I went forward to give my life to Christ.

I know that not all conversions are dramatic—but mine was. I went home thrilled and astonished, like a boy who had rubbed a lamp and found a real genie inside. I had always believed in Jesus Christ the way a child believes in Santa Claus or the Easter bunny. But I never believed he was *real* until I met him that night. I drove home elated and went to bed knowing my life would never be the same again.

Yet when I awoke the next morning, everything *was* the same. I expected to feel the glow of God's presence the way I had the night before, but I didn't feel anything. Alarmed, I fell to my knees and prayed, "Lord, *where are you?* I thought you entered my life last night and that you would still be with me in the morning." No answer. Nothing but silence. I felt like a newlywed who had awakened to find that his bride had left him.

For nearly a month I searched for the Lord, wondering why he seemed so far away, when we had known such intimacy the night of my conversion.

I kept hoping that the person who counseled me at the Billy Graham movie would call so that I could ask for his help, but he never did—or so I thought. I didn't find out until years later, while I was in seminary, that every time he tried to get in touch with me, my father would go to the phone and say, "I don't want you calling here. Leave my son alone!"

Because I didn't have a church, I went with my next-door neighbor to an Episcopal priest to get his advice. But when I asked him whether we should always feel the presence of the Lord, he said, "It sounds to me like you've been talking with some Holy Rollers!"

I even remember drinking beer with some of my high school buddies and wondering whether the "high" I felt was at all related to the feeling I had the night of my conversion. It sounds almost blasphemous now, but I was only seventeen and I couldn't figure out what it meant to be a Christian.

Finally I decided I was through. Feeling like a jilted lover, I went upstairs to bed one evening to tell the Lord good-bye.

The light on the nightstand was still on in the room, and my younger brother, Gary, was asleep in the twin bed next to mine. I crawled under the covers, laid my head back on the pillow, and began my "Dear John" prayer to the Lord.

I don't remember the exact words, but they were something like the following: "Heavenly Father, I have done everything I can to try to find you, but you haven't been willing to help me. I don't know what else to do! Why won't you—"

My prayer was cut short in mid-sentence. Suddenly, in ever-increasing intensity, the holy presence of the Lord began to fill and surround me. Ezekiel speaks of the time when "the cloud filled the temple, and the court was full of the radiance of the glory of the Lord." Although there was no cloud around my bed, that same glory radiated within me, and holy love permeated every part of my being.

My mind raced and my breathing quickened, not from fear, but because the God of the universe had pulled back the curtain that separates heaven and earth and was in my room—my *heart!* All that I could utter was "Father."

Please understand that I am not describing a "feeling" or emotion, although I have never felt so elated and completely fulfilled as I did during those moments. Rather I am describing the real presence of God, who for some reason revealed himself to me in a special way that night. The emotions I felt were simply a response to him.

It's difficult to recall how long this experience lasted. Two minutes? Five? All I know is that when the Lord had fulfilled his purposes, the glory gradually subsided.

I understand now why John writes that "God is love" rather than "God is loving." For the presence I felt that evening was love—glorious, holy love—the One whom we have longed for our entire lives, even when we thought we were seeking someone or something else. As a result of that experience, I know too that heaven is not primarily a place but a person.

The Lord did not speak to me audibly, but I was left with a definite impression that I believe was from him. I realized that he *had* been with me all along, even when I could not feel his presence. I also understood that I could not possibly function if I always felt his presence the way I did that night—the glorious presence that is within every Christian but that must be concealed during our brief time on earth.

You may be wondering why God needed to assure me personally of his presence, when he has already given us that assurance in his Word. I don't have a good answer to that question. I do know that the only Bible we had in our home was a Gideon Bible my father had taken from a hotel, and I had only read a few chapters in it. In fact, when I was told the night of my conversion to go home and read the Gospel of John, it took me ten minutes just to find it! God saw my need and simply had mercy on me.

That was thirty years ago. And although I have longed for and prayed to have that experience again, the Lord has never answered my prayer—at least, not in the way that I have asked.

I believe that many Christians feel the frustration I felt as a new Christian. The Bible assures us of God's presence and power, but we often feel as if he is on vacation in Acapulco. This feeling seems most acute when we ask him to deliver us from difficulties, hardships, or personal weaknesses and he doesn't seem to answer.

The Lord can certainly reveal himself to us in a dramatic way, just as he did to me on that unforgettable evening. Deep in our hearts, we wish he would *always* respond in that way, whether we are seeking assurance of his presence or needing a fresh display of his power.

It seems so simple really, if God would only cooperate! When we are sick, God should instantly make us well. When we have a financial need, he should send us money in the mail (or let us win the Publishers Clearinghouse Sweepstakes). And if we become unemployed, he should find us a better and higher-paying job.

Like the prophet Isaiah, we cry out, "Oh, that you would rend the heavens and come down, that the mountains would tremble before you! As when fire sets twigs ablaze and causes water to boil, come down to make your name known!" We want God to demolish the obstacles we face and to transform all our weaknesses into strengths.

But our ways are not God's ways, Isaiah reminds us, and our thoughts are not his thoughts. If we demand that God conform his ways to ours, we are bound to be disappointed. If we insist that he measure up to our worldly concepts of power, then we will eventually become disillusioned and filled with doubt.

We need a new perspective. If Isaiah is right and God's thoughts are not our thoughts, then the truth should catch us off guard. And if God's ways are not our ways, then we should find his strength where we least expect it. That premise is the starting point and guiding principle of this book.

1

I Wish I Were Superman

Faster than a speeding bullet. More powerful than a loco-motive. Able to leap tall buildings in a single bound. "Look, up in the sky! Is it a bird? Is it a plane?" No, it's Superman! Strange visitor from another planet, who came to earth with powers and abilities far beyond those of mortal men. Superman. Who can change the course of mighty rivers, bend steel in his bare hands. And who, disguised as Clark Kent, mild-mannered reporter for a great metropolitan news-paper, fights a never-ending battle for truth, justice, and the American way!

I first saw *The Amazing Adventures of Superman* on television when I was three years old. Although it took me a few thrill-packed episodes to realize that Clark Kent and Superman were the same person (the glasses had me fooled completely), I was hooked immediately. After all, what kid wouldn't want to be able to fly through the air like a bird, have bullets bounce off his chest, or pick up his parents' car with one hand?

All of our towels were twisted and wrinkled at the corners, because I would tie them around my neck and fly through the house. Finally my mother made me a little red cape with the special Superman **S** on the back. Now I no longer wanted to *be* Superman; I *was* Superman!

When the apostle Paul became a man, he put away childish things. Not me! When *Superman: The Movie* came out a few years ago, I was one of the first ones to see it. And when Christopher Reeve first put on that suit and flew up to save Lois Lane, I was cheering with everyone else. Even after all those years, Superman was still my hero.

You would think that I would have felt embarrassed, a grown man sitting there in the theater with a bunch of kids. But guess what! Most of the people in the audience were adults like me who were reliving their childhood fantasy. In fact, I'm surprised that any kids were able to get tickets for those first few showings.

What is it about the Superman myth that has so captured our culture? What makes a grown man want to pull open the buttons on his shirt to reveal the Superman symbol?

For one thing, it would be a lot of *fun* to be Superman.

Flying would be the best part. I would love to be able to take three or four steps, jump into the air, and keep right on going! Wouldn't it be great to be "faster than a speeding bullet," to fly beside a 747 and wave at the pilot for a moment before you leave him in your vapor trail?

I would also enjoy being able to grab the empty and useless gun out of a bad guy's hand and then do the really cool Superman thing—bend the barrel like a pretzel. And X-ray vision would be nice, although I would only use it in the service of humanity, of course. Perhaps Superman simply embodies our idea of a really good time.

But for me at least (and I suspect for many others), Superman represents more than fun—much more.

MORE POWERFUL THAN A LOCOMOTIVE

While Superman was still an infant on his native planet, Krypton, his father began to prepare a space capsule that would take him on the long journey to Earth. Just before little Kal-el was put into the capsule, his parents argued the pros and cons of his future:

> *Lehra:* He will defy their gravity.
>
> *Jor-el:* He will look like one of them.
>
> *Lehra:* He won't *be* one of them.
>
> *Jor-el:* No, his dense molecular structure will make him *strong.*[1]

Later as the child's capsule plunges into Earth's atmosphere like a fiery meteor, it burns a path across a field in the town of Smallville, home of Jonathan and Martha Kent. As they retrieve the boy from his charred vessel and bring him back to their truck, they soon discover his amazing powers. While Jonathan is fixing a flat tire, the jack suddenly gives way. Martha screams as the truck starts to fall on her husband, but it never reaches the ground. Their little Superboy is holding it up above his head with an innocent grin on his face.

That's just the beginning. In high school, young Clark kicks a football so hard that it goes hundreds of feet into the air. Then on the way home he decides to show off and runs faster than a train.

When he finally grows up, Superman is so strong that he can catch a falling helicopter in one hand while he holds a breathless Lois Lane in the other. He can chase a runaway missile and hurl it into outer space. And he can even lift millions of tons of rock and dirt in order to repair the San Andreas Fault. What a guy!

Superman embodies our desire to be strong and powerful. We may not want to bend steel in our bare hands, but strength and power are great assets in almost every other area of life.

Throughout their school years, boys and girls are thrust into athletic competition. There they quickly learn that victory goes to the fastest runners, the longest hitters, and the strongest players.

I still have painful memories of the two years that I played high school football. I joined the team because athletes were the most popular kids I knew, not because I really wanted to play. I assumed that our daily workouts would consist mainly of playing catch, kicking the ball a few times, and having a friendly practice game now and then.

Wrong. Little did I know that football practice is the high school equivalent of boot camp. We started with workouts twice a day under the sweltering sun and one-hundred-degree heat of a Texas summer. We learned the joy of running till you drop or puke—or preferably both. At lunchtime we would go home soaking wet, covered in scabs and bruises and scrapes, and then we'd come back in the afternoon for more of the same. If you had masochistic tendencies, it was great! (I didn't.)

I felt like a midget among a bunch of house apes. I only weighed about one hundred and fifty pounds, while the best players weighed from one hundred seventy to over two hundred pounds. But what I lacked in size, I also lacked in speed. Even some of the linemen—the kind who make the earth shake when they run—could beat me in a race. And to make matters worse, I didn't have the face of a football player. Other players could look really mean and intimidating, while I looked sweet and nice and had sort of an "easy meat" expression that really appealed to the carnivores on our team.

I'll never forget one particular practice. During one of our drills, they had us get into two lines, with those at the front of each line about ten yards apart. The coach would throw the ball to a person in one line, and then the two players would try to have a head-on collision in the middle.

When my turn came, I was standing opposite one of the biggest, meanest linemen on our team. Instead of throwing the ball directly to me, the coach deliberately threw it high into the air so that I would have to reach up to catch it. The moment my fingers touched the ball, the lineman smashed into my exposed chest and brought me crashing to the ground. As I lay there humiliated and gasping for breath, one thought entered my mind—*I wish I were Superman!*

Yet strength is more than size or big muscles. I would also love to have Superman's energy and stamina, especially now that I have reached middle age. Someone once said of Howard Hendricks, one of my seminary professors, that he ran on 220 volts, while all the other professors ran on 110 volts. If that were true, then my energy rating would be about 9 volts—just enough to power a smoke detector or a calculator but certainly not enough for a grown man. My wife isn't much better.

We had our children late in life, so they are only seven and eight years old. They have so much energy that we can't keep up with them. When I come home from the office tired and ready to relax, they want to go to the park, go on a bike ride, play hide-and-seek and a dozen other games. Recently as we had just finished a marathon of activity and they were taking turns jumping and bouncing on Daddy, I thought to myself—*I wish I were Superman!*

ABLE TO LEAP TALL BUILDINGS

Superman also appeals to our desire for achievement. Have you ever noticed that nothing is too hard for Superman? No challenge is too difficult; no obstacle is too great. He has all of the personal resources he needs to do *anything* he wants to do.

A massive earthquake threatens to make California drop into the Pacific Ocean? No problem. Superman merely zips up the San Andreas Fault. A fire at a chemical plant may cause a massive explosion? Don't worry. Superman simply freezes a lake with his supercold breath, lifts the ice into the air, and then uses it to put out the blaze. And when Lois Lane is crushed to death in her car, Superman even responds to the ultimate challenge. In a strange twist on Einstein's theory of relativity, Superman flies nearly the speed of light and causes time to go *backward* so that he can return to earth before Lois's accident even occurred. Superman seldom needs anyone's help—in heaven or on earth—to get the job done.

That's a far cry from the little poem *The Impossible Thing:*

> They said it couldn't be done.
>> They said no one could get through it.
> So I decided to tackle that impossible thing.
>> And guess what: I couldn't do it!

Most of us face challenges that are beyond our abilities. I'm not talking at this point about what God can do with us and through us—that will come in later chapters—but rather about our natural limitations as human beings. Perhaps you always wanted to be a movie star, a professional athlete, a scientist, or even president of the United States. Ever since I saw the movie *Top Gun*, I have thought about the glamour of being a fighter pilot. But I don't think they are interested in recruiting a forty-five-year-old man with a tummy. It's just not going to happen.

I know that the human-potential movement says we can become anything we want to be if we only think positively and set our mind to it. But even if our potential is greater than what we have realized, we don't all have the talent of a movie star or the agility of an athlete or the mind of a scientist. And no amount of positive thinking will change that fact.

In a story called *A Day in the Life of Clarence Bunsen*, Garrison Keillor describes an older man who realizes that the years have slipped away and he hasn't achieved very much. At first Clarence goes to see Father Emil at Our Lady of Perpetual Responsibility Catholic Church for a second opinion (Clarence is Lutheran). When that doesn't help, he takes a walk past the school and climbs the hill overlooking Lake Wobegon, the hill where he and the other kids used to play years ago.

While he is remembering his childhood and reflecting on his life, Clarence hears some kids coming up the path. Then for some strange reason he runs ahead of them and climbs up an old tree that he and the others had nailed sticks to years before. (The climbing wasn't as easy as it used to be!)

The kids stop near the base of the tree, knowing that he is around there someplace, but they don't think to look up. Keillor writes that Clarence "knew that if he jumped down or just said 'Ha!' they'd all jump out of their shoes." Then as Clarence watched them further, he thought to himself:

> I wish I could be like that. I just seem to go through life with my eyes closed and my ears shut.

People talk to me, and I don't even hear them. Whole days go by, and I can't remember what happened. The woman I've lived with for thirty-six years, if you asked me to describe her, I'd have to stop and think about it. It's like I've lived half my life waiting for life to begin, thinking it's somewhere off in the future, and now I'm thinking all the time about death. It's time to live, time to wake up and do something. And he jumped, and he yelled, "Hayee!"

Oh, those boys exploded out of there, like birds! And he said, "Haah!" And then he said, "Ouch! Oooh!"

They came back where he was sitting and said, "You all right, Uncle Clarence?"

He said, "Yes. But go down and tell Mrs. Bunsen to bring the car up to the gravel road. I'll meet her up by the mailbox."

He crawled a hundred yards over to the road. She picked him up; she didn't ask what happened.[2]

It's difficult to know exactly what would have been going through Clarence's mind at that moment as he thought about his sprained ankle, his faded dreams, and his fifty-five-year-old body. But I know what I would have been thinking—I wish I were Superman!

ABILITIES FAR BEYOND THOSE OF MORTAL MEN

Early in life we discover that people with outstanding abilities are both admired and rewarded. Great athletes receive multimillion-dollar contracts and are treated like royalty. Pop singers make obscene amounts of money and have thousands of adoring fans. Financial wizards build lucrative business empires and wield enormous power. Those who have brilliant minds earn scholarships for their education and large grants for later research. And from childhood on, people who are physically attractive gain an edge in most areas over those who are average or plain.

Superman embodies our desire to be noticed, admired, and respected. Because he has "powers and abilities far beyond those of mortal men," he is not only super—he's nearly perfect in every way. His intelligence and education would put an Einstein to shame. After all, during his journey to Earth, his father taught him most of the facts in the known universe. Superman could play on any professional baseball, basketball, or football team and single-handedly win every game. In a conversation with his earthly father, Superman once informed him: "If I wanted to, I could make a touchdown every time I got the ball." And, of course, Superman is incredibly handsome. When Lois Lane interviews him on the terrace of her apartment, the first question she asks him is, "Are you married?" And then, "Do you have a girl-friend?"

But Superman is more than just brilliant, athletic, and superattractive. As we listen in on the interview, we discover just how great he really is:

Lois: How tall are you?

Superman: About six four.

Lois: How much do you weigh?

Superman: Around two twenty-five.

Lois: Is it true that you can see through anything?

Superman: Yes, I can, pretty much.

Lois: And that you're totally impervious to pain?

Superman: Well, so far.[3]

We also learn that he never drinks—at least not while he's flying—he never lies, and he's devoted to fighting for "truth, justice, and the American way."

No wonder we want to be Superman. He is so superior in every way that women swoon over him, men respect him, and kids want to be like him when they grow up. He embodies all of the worldly values that bring fame and glory.

Take the fact that he's tall, dark, and handsome. Our culture has an obsession with being attractive. Look on the cover of any magazine and you'll see someone who is not only drop-dead beautiful but who also has had every flaw airbrushed away. During a recent special on television, I learned that the top ad agencies spend hundreds, even thousands, of dollars making sure that every wrinkle becomes smooth, every blemish is erased, and every trace of fat is trimmed. Finally when perfection is achieved, this image of this ideal woman or man is stuck in front of our faces to remind us of what we should strive to attain. So we rush out to buy the latest makeup, we put ourselves on crash diets, we go to aerobics classes. And when all else fails, we get liposuction to remove bulges where we don't want them, silicone implants to get bulges where we do want them, and cosmetic surgery to remove one or more of our extra chins. Deep down inside, if we're honest, we must realize that it's never going to happen—we will *never* look as good as Christopher Reeve or Cindy Crawford. But we keep on trying anyway. If only we could look slimmer, stronger, younger, flatter, smoother, and more attractive—then maybe people would notice and admire us. What a sad pursuit!

THE MAN OF STEEL

Last of all, but perhaps most importantly, Superman represents our desire for security. We live in an uncertain world, one that can shatter our tranquil existence at any moment.

Not long ago a friend of mine was asked by his supervisor to come into a conference room. When they both emerged a few minutes later, my friend had been laid off. There was absolutely no warning. He had worked for the company for seven years and always had excellent job reviews. He was doing what he had been hired to do, and he had the company's approval for every project he was working on. His department was not even behind budget. Yet in the space of a brief conversation, his world was turned upside down.

Of course, his situation is far from unique. In our country alone there are 8.7 million people who are unemployed. Every day thousands of people lose their jobs and face the possibility of financial hardship or ruin.

This would never happen to Superman. Although he never claims to be rich, I still remember one of his most impressive feats in *The Amazing Adventures of Superman*. In one episode Clark Kent, Lois Lane, and

Jimmy Olsen are in Africa when some bad guys steal a large diamond from an idol worshiped by the natives. Just when it seems that there is no hope and the three of them will be boiled in a large cast-iron pot, Clark secretly picks up a lump of coal, squeezes it in his hand until smoke appears, and compresses the coal into a large diamond—just like the one that had been stolen from the natives. No one who can do a trick like that ever needs to worry about unemployment or welfare!

The best most people can do is hope to win the lottery, and millions of dollars are wasted every week—usually by those who can least afford to waste money—in the pursuit of financial security.

Yet even if we could win the lottery or be as wealthy as Solomon himself, we would still not be secure.

A few weeks ago a friend of ours was diagnosed with breast cancer. When the doctor went to remove the cancer, he found that it had entered her lymph nodes, and she is now undergoing chemotherapy. Although her prognosis is hopeful, there are no guarantees that she will recover.

When I spoke with her husband a day or so after the cancer was discovered, he said, "You know, just yesterday our family was so happy and peaceful and content. Now overnight everything has changed."

Cancer or other illnesses could never threaten Superman. His father declared that he would be "practically invulnerable," and Lois discovered that he is "impervious to pain." Except for an occasional bout with Kryptonite, Superman's one weakness, he is virtually immortal.

Several months ago my wife discovered a small lump on my back. This was only a week or two after a good friend of ours had died of stomach cancer. Even though I hoped for the best, I was really scared and concerned as I went into the doctor's office. I kept wondering whether I would ever get to see my children grow up and whether I too would be dead in a few months just like our friend. Although I prayed and tried to trust in the Lord during that time, my old secret longing returned—*I wish I were Superman!*[4]

There is nothing wrong with our desire for safety and security. For that matter, there is nothing wrong with wanting to be strong, energetic, successful, admired, attractive, or even immortal. The Scriptures teach that when Jesus returns we will be all of these things and more. Yet in a fallen world our desire for power and greatness can take a sinister twist—what I call "the Superman syndrome"—and those who achieve these goals face two deadly perils that the Lord hates and will not tolerate. We will begin to explore these dangers and their remedy in the following chapter.

2

GOD LOVES NINETY-POUND WEAKLINGS

The original Arnold Schwarzenegger was a man named Charles Atlas. As a kid, I remember seeing his bodybuilding ads at the back of magazines. With his bulging muscles and leopard-skin Speedo suit, Atlas seemed like the pinnacle of manhood. Sometimes he would pose with a shapely young beauty cradled in his arms. The look on his face seemed to say, "If you only had muscles like mine, you too could pick up good-looking girls!"

Yet his most famous ad showed a "ninety-pound weakling" sitting on the beach with his girlfriend. While the couple sat minding their own business, along came a big bully, who laughed at the skinny runt and kicked sand in his face.

That humiliating experience, plus a strong desire for revenge, was all that the ninety-pound weakling needed.

He sent off for Charles Atlas' book of bodybuilding secrets, lifted weights, did push-ups and sit-ups, and then reappeared on the beach with his own leopard-skin Speedo suit and a new, muscular body. In the final frame of the ad, the former weakling confronted the bully. I can't recall whether he beat the bully to a pulp or merely kicked sand in *his* face, but I do remember that the results were very satisfying.

Unfortunately I never did send off for the book. I can still wear V-shaped athletic-build shirts and suits, however, but only if I put them on upside down!

Throughout our lives, we often view ourselves and others as either ninety-pound weaklings or as Charles Atlases. Of course, you don't need to have bulging muscles to be a Charles Atlas. He symbolizes the elite members of our society—those who are powerful, rich, famous, and attractive.

We see such people everywhere, not just on TV or in magazines. They pull up beside us in their Mercedes or Acura Legends, talking on their cellular phones. We drive by their oversized homes with three-car garages and manicured lawns. We see them at work in their power suits and corner offices. They are the people who are climbing the social and corporate ladder, who are fulfilling the American Dream.

If we are honest, we have to admit that most of us do not fall into the Charles Atlas category. We may not view ourselves as ninety-pound weaklings, but we often envy the rich and famous and long to be like them. And why shouldn't we? Who in their right mind wouldn't prefer success to failure, strength to weakness, fame to obscurity, and wealth to poverty? No wonder many Christians make power, fame, riches, and success their ultimate goals in life and assume that the Lord wants to help them achieve these goals.

When I first became a Christian, I assumed that God was sort of a divine Charles Atlas who would teach me the secrets of spiritual bodybuilding. No more skinny runt! No more sand kicked in my face! Now, with God's help and blessing, I would get rid of all my weaknesses and exchange them for strengths. But imagine my shock and surprise when I discovered that God *prefers* ninety-pound weaklings.

THE REVENGE OF THE NERDS

In his first letter to the Corinthians, Paul asks his readers to consider what types of people attend their church:

> Brothers, think of what you were when you were called. Not many of you were wise by human standards; not many were influential; not many were of noble birth. But God chose the foolish things of the world to shame the wise; God chose the weak things of the world to shame the strong. He chose the lowly things of this world and the despised things—and the things that are not—to nullify the things that are. (1 Cor. 1:26–28)

According to Paul, the congregation at Corinth was filled with plain, ordinary people, those whom Paul describes as "the foolish," "the weak," "the lowly," and "the despised." This motley crew also included "the things that are not," which could be paraphrased as "the nobodies." Very few "somebodies"—those who were wise, influential, or of noble birth—had put their faith in Christ and joined the church.

Because the Corinthians lived two thousand years ago, the profile of their church doesn't bother us. We may even feel grateful that God was willing to save such people. But our attitude changes completely if we transfer that profile to our church, Christian group, or circle of friends. We not only long to be powerful and successful ourselves, we also like to be seen in the company of such people. And we often measure success or failure by standards that God rejects. Let me illustrate what I mean.

When I was a freshman at the University of Texas, I remember visiting two Christian groups on campus. The first group was by far the most popular. They met weekly at the posh Student Alumni Center. When I entered the door, two attractive coeds greeted me and asked if I would like to sign up for a door prize. Then they ushered me into a large room filled with over two hundred students.

As I looked around the room I realized that most of the students represented the campus elite. They were the fraternity and sorority crowd, the football players, cheerleaders, and student council members. If someone had deliberately sought out the most beautiful and powerful people on campus, they could not have come up with a better group.

In fact, somebody had. This particular campus ministry told their staff members to actively recruit those at the top of the social heap. Their philosophy was that if they could win for Christ those who were attractive, athletic, or influential, then other, "lesser" students would also want to join the group.

In order to make their strategy work, they brought in the big guns, an army of staff members who looked like they were hired from a modeling agency. The men could have got a second job posing for the cover of *GQ* magazine, and the women could have given most beauty contestants a run for their money.

Yet they were more than attractive. As soon as they stepped to the front of the room and began leading the meeting, I realized that they were also bright, talented, energetic, and capable of putting on a first-class show. I was dazzled!

A few nights later I visited the other group. They met in an ugly, sterile-looking classroom complete with chalkboard and desks. There were only thirty or so students present, and if a casting director had been looking for prospects to star in *The Revenge of the Nerds*, he couldn't have come to a better place. Instead of being greeted by cute coeds, I was welcomed by a tall, skinny guy with glasses, who talked too loud and laughed at his own jokes. Then I was introduced to their one itinerant staff member, a short, mousy-looking fellow with horn-rimmed glasses and weird hair.

Their program was about as flashy as the people themselves. We watched a promotional film about an upcoming missionary conference—not exactly prime-time material!

Whenever there are two such groups on campus, people are bound to compare them, or in this case to contrast them. By virtually every earthly standard, the first group was clearly superior. They had more staff, more people, more campus leaders, more converts, more *everything*. About the only area they would have conceded to the second group was that they were more "intellectual." Yet this was sort of a backhanded compliment, like telling someone that his blind date has "a good personality." What they really meant was that the second group was a bunch of geeks and losers. Without anyone realizing it, worldly standards of success and failure were being used to evaluate these two works of God and the people associated with them.[1]

I believe that these same standards have infected the church at large. Because I work in the Christian publishing industry, I see signs of this infection every day. Our industry is dominated by those who are "spiritual superstars," whose flamboyant styles and outgoing personalities make them the darlings of the Christian media. People buy their books and flock to their seminars, not because of the quality of their message but because they are *celebrities*—Christians who have attained the same degree of fame, power, and success as their secular counterparts.

Of course, we should be thankful when anyone comes to faith in Christ, including those near the top of the social, economic, or political spectrum. Yet I believe that our celebrity worship and our tendency to define greatness in terms of popularity, power, wealth, education, or beauty is profoundly unbiblical and even dangerous. When we fawn over such people and make them our role models and standards of success, our attitude is the exact opposite of the Lord's!

If I understand Paul correctly, the Corinthian church is a microcosm of the church at large. Throughout history, those who are foolish, weak, lowly, and insignificant have eagerly embraced Jesus Christ and the Gospel, while most of the elite have turned up their noses and walked away.

Although we might be tempted to blame ourselves for this imbalance and to view it as a failure in our evangelism, Paul attributes it to God's sovereign choice. The Lord deliberately chose the foolish people of the world "to shame the wise." He chose the weak people of the world "to shame the strong." He chose the lowly people of this world and the despised people "to nullify the things that are." In other words, the Lord's long-range goal is to make the somebodies of this world into nobodies and the nobodies into somebodies!

Why would he want to do this? Why would God want to shame the elite, when everyone else wants to honor them? Why would he want to bring them down, when everyone else wants to put them on a pedestal?

The answer can be summed up in one word—pride. Paul tells us that God intends "to nullify the things that are, so that no one may boast before him." Lord Acton is well known for his statement that power corrupts, and absolute power corrupts absolutely. Yet he never explained why this is so. The Bible leaves no doubt about the reason. Power, wealth, and fame usually lead to pride, one of the attitudes that God despises most.

YERTLE THE TURTLE

Dr. Seuss wrote a children's story called *Yertle the Turtle* that illustrates the dangers of pride. In the story, Yertle is ruler of a little pond on the faraway Island of Sala-ma-Sond. Dr. Seuss tells us:

> The turtles had everything turtles might need. And they were all happy. Quite happy indeed. They *were* . . . until Yertle, the king of them all, decided the kingdom he ruled was too small.
>
> "I'm ruler," said Yertle, "of all that I see. But I don't see *enough*. That's the trouble with me. With this stone for a throne, I look down on my pond, but I cannot look down on the places beyond. This throne that I sit on is too, too low down. It ought to be *higher!*" he said with a frown. "If I could sit high, how much greater I'd be! What a king! I'd be ruler of all I could see!"

In his quest for greatness, Yertle ordered some of the turtles in the pond to stand on each other's backs so that they could become his new and higher throne. Soon he had a wonderful view and could see "most a mile." Yet Yertle wasn't satisfied. He ordered more and more turtles to become part of his throne so that he could be exalted to even greater heights. From his lofty perch, Yertle swelled with stupid pride and feelings of self-importance:

> "All mine!" Yertle cried. "Oh, the things I now rule! I'm king of a cow! And I'm king of a mule! I'm king of a house! And, what's more beyond that, I'm king of a blueberry bush and a cat! I'm Yertle the

Turtle! Oh, marvelous me! For I am the ruler of all that I see!"

Then something happened at the bottom of his turtle throne. One insignificant subject named Mack decided that he and the other turtles had taken enough abuse. He didn't organize a rebellion, however; he merely *burped*. Yet the tremors from that burp brought down the mighty Yertle and plunged him into the place reserved for all who think they are something special: "And today the great Yertle, that Marvelous he, is King of the Mud. That is all he can see."[2]

The corrupting influences of power are not limited to storybook turtles. Paul identifies three groups of people who in every generation, including our own, are prime candidates for pride. They are "the strong," "the wise," and those "of noble birth." As we look at each group, we will discover why life at the top can be so dangerous.

THE STRONG

In ancient Babylon, Yertle had a human counterpart in King Nebuchadnezzar, the ruler of the largest and most powerful nation on earth. At the height of his reign, Nebuchadnezzar did what most powerful people do. He began to boast of his accomplishments and to take full credit for them:

> As the king was walking on the roof of the royal palace of Babylon, he said, "Is not this the great Babylon I have built as the royal residence, by my mighty power and for the glory of my majesty?"

The words were still on his lips when a voice came from heaven, "This is what is decreed for you, King Nebuchadnezzar: Your royal authority has been taken from you. You will be driven away from people and will live with the wild animals; you will eat grass like cattle. Seven [years] will pass by for you until you acknowledge that the Most High is sovereign over the kingdoms of men and gives them to anyone he wishes." (Dan. 4:29–32)

Actually, the statement "and gives them to anyone he wishes" is a milder form of what God said earlier. When Daniel first confronted Nebuchadnezzar, he tried to burst the king's bubble of pride by saying, "The Most High is sovereign over the kingdoms of men and gives them to anyone he wishes and *sets over them the lowliest of men*"(Dan. 4:17, emphasis added).

Usually those at the top—or on their way to the top—think they are something special, that they are superior to mere mortals. Like Nebuchadnezzar, they believe that their own "mighty power" is responsible for their achievements, and they begin to glorify themselves rather than glorifying God.

To all such people, God gives the ultimate put-down. They are dead wrong when they assume that they are something special—in fact, they may be "the lowliest of men." And they occupy their position—at least for the moment—not because of their own power and glory but because of God's sovereign choice, a choice he can revoke at any time.

After being cast down from his throne and having lost his sanity for seven years, mighty King Nebuchadnezzar, the Yertle of Babylon, learned his lesson. At the conclusion of the story, he proclaims, "Now I, Nebuchadnezzar, praise and exalt and glorify the King of heaven, because everything he does is right and all his ways are just." Then with considerable understatement he adds, "And those who walk in pride he is able to humble."

Paul tells us that "God chose the weak things of the world to shame the strong." We need to hear both the warning and the hope in his words. Those who become so strong that they feel no need of God will ultimately get their wish, but not as they imagined. Their "glory" will be turned into shame, and their great power will be powerless to save them. But those who are "weak," who humbly admit their need for God's help and daily strength, will find that they have been granted the only power that matters—the power of God.

THE WISE

The second group Paul mentions includes "the wise," "the scholar," and "the philosopher." In our day he might also have added "the scientist" and "the university professor." Such people are the intellectual elite, the great minds that shape our thinking and provide us with new technologies.

Paul is not being anti-intellectual, as some fundamentalists have mistakenly assumed. Paul himself was a rabbinic scholar, and Festus, the governor of Judea, referred to Paul's "great learning" (Acts 26:24). Nor is Paul saying that scientists and scholars cannot be

Christians. Although there were not many of "the wise" at Corinth, there were some, and throughout history many great minds have accepted Jesus Christ, including such notables as Galileo Galilei, Sir Isaac Newton, and Johannes Kepler.

But for the most part, the "wisdom" of scholars, philosophers, and scientists has led them away from God rather than toward him. As Paul writes elsewhere, they are "always learning but never able to acknowledge the truth" (2 Tim. 3:7).

I was probably one of the last people on earth to read Stephen Hawking's book *A Brief History of Time*, a book that was on everyone's "must read list" for several months. Hawking is considered to be the most brilliant theoretical physicist since Einstein. *Time* magazine said of him, "Even as he sits helpless in his wheelchair, his mind seems to soar ever more brilliantly across the vastness of space and time to unlock the secrets of the universe."

Yet surely the greatest "secret of the universe" is God himself, the One who created everything. And those who study the universe most carefully, as Hawking has done, should be confronted by the evidence of God's existence everywhere they look. After all, the psalmist tells us that "the heavens declare the glory of God; the skies proclaim the work of his hands" (Ps. 19:1). The beauty, grandeur, and intricacy of creation reveal God's glory to anyone willing to see, and they declare his handiwork to anyone willing to listen.

I was profoundly disappointed, therefore, to discover that Hawking's universe has no place for God.

Although Hawking discusses God frequently, the foreword by Carl Sagan sums up the author's conclusions:

> This is also a book about God ... or perhaps about the absence of God. The word God fills these pages. Hawking embarks on a quest to answer Einstein's famous question about whether God had any choice in creating the universe. Hawking is attempting, as he explicitly states, to understand the mind of God. And this makes all the more unexpected the conclusion of the effort, at least so far: a universe with no edge in space, no beginning or end in time, and nothing for a Creator to do.[3]

Nothing for a Creator to do in his own universe? Not exactly, for both Hawking and Sagan are claiming that there is no need for a Creator. What arrogance! If that is the best that their brilliant minds can do, I would rather conclude that there is no need for Hawking and Sagan! Their so-called wisdom is really the ultimate folly.

And that, of course, is Paul's point. Because so many "wise" men and scholars and philosophers have missed the most important fact in the universe, they are really the greatest of fools. And the most "foolish" people on earth, who know Jesus Christ and little else, are actually the most wise.

THE NOBLE

The third group Paul mentions are those "of noble birth," whom he also describes as "the things that are"—the somebodies, the elite members of society.

In English the word *noble* can mean "possessing superiority of ... character or of ideals or morals" or it can mean "of high birth or exalted rank."[4] Clearly the two definitions have no necessary connection, for some people of high birth or exalted rank are quite immoral and unscrupulous. How then did a word that means superiority of character come to be applied to "the nobility"? My guess is that they applied it to themselves!

Yet here I must exercise caution, lest I be accused of disrespect. In Oscar Wilde's play *The Importance of Being Ernest*, Lady Bracknell says to her nephew, "Do not speak disrespectfully of Society, Algernon. Only people who cannot get into it do that!"

Yet *getting into it* is precisely the problem and the goal to which most people aspire. In an essay entitled "The Inner Ring," C. S. Lewis writes, "I believe that in all men's lives at certain periods, and in many men's lives at all periods between infancy and extreme old age, one of the most dominant elements is the desire to be inside the local Ring and the terror of being left outside." He goes on to say that

> this desire, in one of its forms, has indeed had ample justice done to it in literature. I mean, in the form of snobbery. Victorian fiction is full of characters who are hagridden by the desire to get inside that particular Ring which is, or was, called Society. But it must be clearly understood that "Society," in that sense of the word, is merely one of a hundred Rings and snobbery, therefore, only one form of the longing to be inside.[4]

Throughout our lives we are confronted by various elite groups whose very existence depends on including some and excluding others. During grade school and middle school, the groups may simply be "us" and "them." In high school they are often referred to as cliques. And in college they are best represented by fraternities and sororities.

As Lewis suggests, we may strive all of our lives to get into these various elite groups. And if we fail to be admitted, we may feel snubbed or inferior to those on the inside.

But consider the grave danger we would face if we were allowed into the inner Ring, whatever form it may take. As with "the strong" and "the wise," the somebodies of this world often feel superior to the nobodies. They often take great pride at being included while others are excluded. And that very pride can drive them farther and farther from God.

Paul tells us not to worry. God "chose the lowly things of this world and the despised things—and the things that are not—to nullify the things that are, so that no one may boast before him." Those who are among the elite or Society or the inner Ring may one day find themselves excluded from the only group that ultimately matters. And the nobodies of this world, who have been snubbed and excluded and looked down on, will find that they have been admitted to the Royal Society of the King of kings.

3

THE STRENGTH OF WEAKNESS

When I was in sixth grade, a friend named Ginny Cole brought her pony over to my house and asked if I wanted to ride. As soon as I got on the pony's back, it bolted forward and ran out of control as fast as it could.

The ride only lasted a few seconds. As we raced around to the back of the house the pony headed straight for a tall, spindly olive tree that was covered with inch-long thorns. Just before we reached the tree, the pony swerved to the right. Unfortunately, I didn't. I flew off its back and, with one hand still gripping the reins, was pulled up and over the olive tree, which bent over double and then snapped back into position.

By the time I hit the ground, thorns had punctured my entire left side. I cried out in pain, and my father ran over to help me. He took me inside the house, gently removed each thorn, and cleaned my wounds. To this day I have several scars that remind me of the worst ride of my life.

Now imagine for a moment that my father had not removed the thorns. Suppose that in spite of my cries and pleas for help he had decided that it was best to leave them in my body. Sounds monstrous and unthinkable, doesn't it? And yet that is exactly what our heavenly Father often chooses to do with the "thorns" that puncture and wound us.

Why would he do such a thing? Why would he withhold the care that even our earthly parents would not hesitate to give? The typical answer is that he wants to develop character in our lives. And, of course, that is true. But as we will discover in this chapter, God has other vitally important reasons for helping us bear the pain rather than removing it.

A THORNY PROBLEM

The apostle Paul knew the pain of being punctured and wounded by thorns. In 2 Corinthians 12:7–10, a passage that has become a biblical classic on suffering, he describes what he calls "a thorn in my flesh." He writes:

> To keep me from becoming conceited … there was given me a thorn in my flesh, a messenger of Satan, to torment me. Three times I pleaded with the Lord to take it away from me. But he said to me, "My grace is sufficient for you, for my power is made perfect in weakness." Therefore I will boast all the more gladly about my weaknesses, so that Christ's power may rest on me. That is why, for

Christ's sake, I delight in weaknesses, in insults, in
hardships, in persecutions, in difficulties. For when
I am weak, then I am strong.

For centuries people have speculated about the pre-
cise nature of Paul's thorn. They have suggested that it
was headaches, earaches, eye disease, or malarial fever.
Others have claimed it was epilepsy, a speech impedi-
ment, hypochondria, deafness, or remorse for perse-
cuting Christians. Still others have suggested gallstones,
gout, rheumatism, a dental infection—even lice![1]

All this scholarly speculation has led to one very
firm conclusion. We don't have a clue about the specific
nature of Paul's thorn! But that really doesn't matter.
Whatever it was, it felt *painful*, like the thorns that
pierced me after my runaway ride in the sixth grade.
Paul says his thorn "tormented" him and made him
plead with God to remove it.

We also know that many other experiences in Paul's
life qualified as "thorns." According to verse 10, these
experiences included a wide variety of weaknesses,
insults, hardships, persecutions, and difficulties. In other
words, a thorn can be almost *anything* difficult or
painful—other than sin, of course—that makes us cry
out to God for help. It might be an illness, a physical
injury, an abusive boss, a financial hardship, a stressful
situation, or any one of a hundred other problems we
face in a fallen world.

Yet to really understand Paul's thorn, it is far more
important to know *why* it was than *what* it was. If we can
discover why God gave Paul his thorn in the flesh, then

we can also know why God often fails to remove the thorns in our lives.

EATING HUMBLE PIE

The first reason is clear: "To keep me from becoming conceited" (v. 7). In the previous chapter we considered the fact that one of God's long-range goals is to make the somebodies of this world into nobodies and the nobodies into somebodies. Because the somebodies of this world usually become proud and boastful, the Lord will ultimately knock them off their pedestal.

But what happens when one of God's own children becomes a "somebody," a person of position, success, fame, or power? In fact, this is what happened to Paul. Spiritually speaking, he made it to the top, to a position of great power and influence. If there had been "corner offices" in the first-century church, Paul's would have been on the top floor, with plush furniture and a beautiful view. After all, Paul was one of Christ's apostles, a member of the elite corps who had seen the risen Lord and who had been personally commissioned by him to preach the gospel.

Paul was also highly successful. He was the greatest evangelist of his day, and some would say of *any* day. He led thousands of people to Christ and planted churches throughout the Roman empire. He was also a highly successful author—to put it modestly. The Lord selected Paul to write Holy Scripture, and under the inspiration of the Spirit he wrote more books than any other New Testament author.

To top it all off, Paul also had incredible spiritual experiences. He spoke in tongues (1 Cor. 14:18), had dreams and visions (Acts 16:6–10), healed the sick (Acts 14:8–10), and was even used by God to raise the dead (Acts 20:7–12). On one very special occasion, he was actually "caught up to the third heaven ... to paradise" and "heard inexpressible things, things that man is not permitted to tell" (2 Cor. 12:1–4).

We have heard these facts so many times that they fail to have their proper impact on us. We are impressed with Billy Graham's gifts of preaching the gospel, or John Stott's ability to teach the Bible, or J. I. Packer's skill in writing theology. But if you put all of these people's gifts together and throw in a John Calvin, a Charles Spurgeon, and a Saint Augustine for good measure, you would only begin to grasp Paul's special anointing by God.

We have heard about Paul's experiences so many times that we also fail to realize their impact on Paul himself. We feel spiritual pride at leading even one person to Christ. Imagine how Paul felt about being the world's greatest evangelist. We would be thrilled if even one article or book we have written gets published. But imagine how Paul felt writing Holy Scripture. We feel close to the Lord when we have a good quiet time. Imagine how Paul felt seeing the Lord face-to-face and being caught up into heaven itself. Pretty heady stuff, even for an apostle!

To keep Paul from soaring aloft with pride, God had to nail his feet to the earth. To keep him from becoming inflated over his accomplishments, God had to burst his bubble. The "thorn" was both the ideal nail and the ideal pin to keep Paul from becoming unbearably conceited.

Whenever *any* of God's children become proud, you can be sure that something will happen to humble them and bring their head back to normal size. Those who are conceited will soon feel the painful prick of a thorn.

Unfortunately, I speak from experience.

One occasion is firmly stuck in my memory. While I was on staff with InterVarsity Christian Fellowship the students at North Texas State University asked me to speak to their group. The topic was "Christ in the Classroom."

I had given this talk at a statewide conference a month earlier and received rave reviews. The students at the conference roared with laughter at my jokes, sat transfixed during my stories, and swarmed me afterward with words of congratulations and appreciation. To be honest, all of that attention and adulation went to my head. I tried to appear humble, but inwardly I was bursting with pride.

Because the students at NTSU were not able to attend that conference, they urged me to speak on the same topic. (My fame had spread all the way to Denton, Texas!) I was ready to dazzle them with my oratory, feeling confident that the very same words would have exactly the same impact they did a month earlier.

I bounded up to the front of the group and launched into my talk. Yet instead of laughing at my jokes, the students sat stone-faced and silent. I tried to captivate them with stories and illustrations, but their minds seemed to be focused on something else. In fact, throughout the talk I sensed an uneasiness in the room that made me wonder what was wrong.

When I finally finished, the president of the student group got up immediately and headed toward me. I thought to myself, *Perhaps my talk went better than it seemed, and he is coming to congratulate me.* But instead he lowered his voice and whispered, "Your zipper is down. It was down the whole time." As I looked up to heaven I thought to myself, *And those who walk in pride he is able to humble.*

Why would God want to humiliate me in front of all those students? Why does he hate pride so much that he would let me wear black slacks and white underwear? Because the Lord will not allow *anyone,* including members of his own family, to take the glory that rightfully belongs to him. Thorns puncture our pride, reminding us and those who might be tempted to glorify us that we are merely human. Thorns take people's focus off the creature and put it on the Creator, where it really belongs.

REWRITING SCRIPTURE

The second reason why God would not remove Paul's thorn is seen in verse 9: "My grace is sufficient for you, for my power is made perfect in weakness." Although this has become one of my favorite verses in Scripture, I have a terrible time accepting what it really says. In fact, if it weren't for the biblical warnings about tampering with Scripture, I would be strongly tempted to rewrite the verse in two ways that would seem far better to me.

One way that would be a real improvement would read, "My grace is sufficient for you, for my power is made perfect by *removing* your weaknesses."

Without realizing it, this is the way many Christians interpret this verse. They expect problems and difficulties and hardships to enter their lives—after all, we live in a fallen world. If they become sick, they expect God to make them well. When they become injured, they expect God to heal them, either naturally or supernaturally. If they encounter a difficulty, either at work or at home, they expect God to resolve it. In whatever area they feel weak, they want God to demonstrate his power by removing their weaknesses. And if he doesn't, at least after a reasonable amount of time, they feel betrayed and begin to wonder whether God really cares about them. For many Christians the presence of God's power equals the absence of problems or weaknesses.

The second way I would like to reword this verse seems even better than the first. What I really want God to say is, "My grace is sufficient for you, for my power will keep you from ever becoming weak."

To be completely honest, I don't want to be weak—*ever*. I want to be so physically strong that I never feel tired, never get sick, never get injured, and never have to face death. I want to be so emotionally strong that I never feel sad, depressed, hurt, or vulnerable. I want to be so rich that I never need to worry about money or the threat of losing my job or whether I will be able to support my family. I want to be so competent that I can face any challenge easily and accomplish any task no matter how difficult. Like Walter Mitty, I sometimes daydream about being such a person, and while the dream lasts it seems like the best life imaginable.

Yet God's statement to Paul in verse 9 shakes me from my slumber and awakens me to the fact that this would not be the best but the *worst* thing that could ever happen to me or to anyone else. Although there is nothing inherently wrong with being strong, rich, secure, or competent, our desires for these things often spring from sinister motives.

Over the years I have learned that my desire to be powerful is really a longing for independence and self-sufficiency. After all, it is frustrating to be weak and dependent on someone else, even if the someone is God himself. In order to depend on God, I need faith—and faith can be risky!

Of course, we evangelicals know in our minds that faith is never really a risk, because God is always faithful to his promises, and his grace is sufficient for any situation. But from a human standpoint, faith *seems* extremely risky.

Let me illustrate what I mean.

I am afraid of heights. I have been known to crawl on my hands and knees to the edge of a high balcony in order to look down. Imagine, then, how I felt when a camp director told me I had to rappel down the side of a steep cliff. "Everybody does it," he said matter-of-factly. "It's part of our program."

With sweaty palms and pounding heart, I eased backward off the edge of the cliff, supported by a rope and a safety line. In order to walk down the face of the cliff, I was told to keep my body perpendicular to the cliff. Every nerve and fiber screamed at me to straighten up, to get in a vertical, not a horizontal, position. Yet those who did so lost their footing and were left dangling high above the ground. Only by fighting my natural urges, and by trusting the ropes and those who held them, did I manage to make it safely to the bottom. What a relief!

That fearful experience of rappelling has become a parable of faith to me. There have been many times in my life when God has asked me to ease over the edge of a cliff, to trust him for something that seemed unsafe and frightening. The primary difference, of course, is that both the safety rope and the person at the top of the cliff are *invisible*—while the cliff and its dangers are in plain sight!

Think about it. Would you be willing to step off a cliff just because someone told you that an invisible hand would hold you and keep you from plunging to your death? Or would you be willing to take off in an airplane with only one wing because someone assured you that God would keep the airplane level? Faith places us in situations where we can only succeed if God keeps up his end of the bargain. Frankly, I would prefer not to have any weaknesses than to take that risk.

The same is true of my desire for financial independence. What I am really saying is that I do not want to depend on God for my daily bread. We live in a day of corporate downsizing, massive layoffs, and frequent restructuring. My father-in-law worked for the same company for over forty years before retiring, but most analysts say those days are gone forever. In such a climate of financial insecurity, I would much rather trust in what I can see—unlimited money in the bank and food on the table—than to rely on God to provide for me and my family.

In other words, if I really got my wish for absolute strength, unlimited wealth, and total competence, I wouldn't feel any need for God. I would never experience his faithfulness or discover his sufficient grace. I would never learn to live in humble dependence on him. I would be tempted to rely on my own power instead of the power of God. In fact, my feelings of pride and self-sufficiency would make me believe I was a god myself.

THE DARKER SIDE OF EDEN

Few of us ever consciously think to ourselves, "Gee, wouldn't it be great if I were a god?" Yet whether consciously or unconsciously, that thought lies beneath the surface of our feelings of pride and self-sufficiency.

When the serpent approached Adam and Eve in the garden, the tempting morsel he dangled in front of them was not just a juicy apple but something far more potent: "God knows that when you eat of it your eyes will be opened, and you will be like God" (Gen. 3:5). Likewise, when the Lord confronted the King of Tyre in Ezekiel 28, he said, "In the pride of your heart you say, 'I am a god; I sit on the throne of a god in the heart of the seas.' But you are a man and not a god, though you think you are as wise as a god" (v. 2). And when the Antichrist comes, Paul tells us that "he will oppose and will exalt himself over everything that is called God or is worshiped, so that he sets himself up in God's temple, proclaiming himself to be God" (2 Thess. 2:4).

Throughout human history, the pharaohs of Egypt, the Caesars of Rome, the emperors of Japan—those whose power, wealth, and prestige made them swell with pride—have claimed for themselves the title of divinity. C. S. Lewis even goes so far as to say, "The essential sin, the utmost evil, is Pride. Unchastity, anger, greed, drunkenness, and all that are mere fleabites in comparison: it was through Pride that the devil became the devil."[2]

So as long as sin remains in the world and in our hearts, we should realize that the thorns in our lives are *friends,* not enemies, because they make us humble rather than proud, dependent rather than independent, and thankful rather than boastful. God does not take sadistic pleasure when his children are pierced and wounded. Nor is he unmoved or unloving when he hears our cries of pain and refuses to remove our thorns. Rather he longs to answer our prayers in the only way they can be answered.

POWER IN WEAKNESS

Paul wants nothing less than a radical reversal in our thinking and behavior. We believe that God's power is best demonstrated by removing our weaknesses or by keeping us from ever becoming weak. Paul tells us that God's power is demonstrated *in the midst of* our weaknesses. We boast about our strengths and believe that strong people have the greatest impact in the world. Paul boasts about his weaknesses, because he realizes that only God's power can accomplish anything of eternal value. We despise our weaknesses and pray for God to take them away. Paul delights in his weaknesses, because they allow him to experience God's incredible power and grace.

For many years I have felt that Joni Eareckson Tada personifies Paul's concept of God's power being perfected in human weakness. In an article in *Moody Monthly*, she writes:

> Our speaker at family camp scanned the audience and said, "I'm tired of hearing that disabled Christians need faith to be healed ... maybe one of those TV healers ought to come here and take a look at *real* miracles of faith!"
>
> Moms and dads of handicapped children erupted in applause. Adults with cerebral palsy struggled to clap. But not in clench-fisted anger. No resentment. Not even a snide, "Yeah, let's show 'em!" The cheers echoed a hearty, "Yes!" to miracles of patience and hard-won endurance. These families experience daily the faith-miracle of God's power showing up best through their weakness.[3]

Joni would be the first to admit that Paul's principle of strength in weakness applies not just to quadriplegics or handicapped children or adults with cerebral palsy. God intends for it to be the normal way of life for *every* Christian—the strong and the weak, the rich and the poor, the somebodies and the nobodies.

The Lord created us to be dependent on him, and when we strive for independence and self-sufficiency, we are fighting a battle that is contrary to our nature and that we can never win.

Because we are mere creatures, we can *never* be strong enough in ourselves to accomplish all that God desires in our lives. And when those who have great physical and emotional strength rely on themselves rather than God, they miss the opportunity to experience a power beyond their comprehension. Even after the Lord returns and we have resurrection bodies that are immortal and imperishable, our power will still be puny in comparison to God's. So is it any wonder that the Lord chooses to display his power rather than ours or to glorify himself rather than us?

God's strength in our weakness—it sounds so simple. Yet there are forces at work in the world and in our hearts that make this simple concept incredibly difficult to learn. In the following chapters we will look at some of these forces and why they tend to dominate our thinking and our behavior. We will also explore how we apply Paul's radical reversal in the most important areas of our lives and ministries.

4

GOD'S WOBBLY WARRIORS

During the mid-seventies, Dallas Theological Seminary produced a promotional brochure called "The Dallas Man." On the front of the brochure were pictured two of the best-looking students on campus. They were standing in front of a fountain, looking cool and confident—and extremely capable.

The promotional copy extolled the virtues of Dallas graduates. They are highly trained Bible expositors, it said, visionary leaders, men of character and substance who could fill any pulpit with distinction. And judging from the two students in the picture, the promotional copy seemed believable. They looked like Supermen in three-piece suits, spiritual Charles Atlases who could kick sand in Satan's face and walk away with the bride of Christ safely in their arms.

I remember discussing the brochure with a fellow student who said, "Well, what did you expect? Should they have used ugly students for models or dressed them in shabby clothes?" At the time, I thought he had a pretty good point, so I dropped the subject and went off to the library to study Greek.

Let me quickly say that I think Dallas Theological Seminary is an excellent institution, and I am thankful for the education and training I received there. Dallas graduates have been used by God throughout the world as pastors, teachers, missionaries, and in a host of other ministries. So my comments are not intended to be a criticism of the seminary or its students.

Still, I think the brochure raises some vitally important questions. What kind of people are most effective in Christian ministry? What qualities should we look for in pastors, teachers, or leaders in Christian organizations? What traits make us the kind of people who can have a powerful impact on the church and the world?

Unfortunately, I think the brochure answered these questions in a way that captures the essence of the Superman syndrome. I mentioned in the previous chapter that faith puts us into situations where we cannot possibly succeed unless God upholds his end of the bargain. Faith joins together the visible and the invisible so that the results cannot adequately be explained apart from God's presence and power.

Yet with the Superman syndrome, what you see is what you get. Not wanting to leave anything to chance or faith, we are tempted to seek powerful, charismatic Christian leaders with a track record that will assure results—whether God is involved or not! Of course, we would never *say* that, but our actions often betray us. In the book *The Evangelical Forfeit*, author John Seel mentions an ad he saw in a national Christian magazine:

> Is your vision to create a contemporary church for the unchurched? Maybe this married, male conservative-evangelical, seminary-graduated baby boomer can help.... Just completed tenure with 4000+ member church ... Master's degrees in Educational Ministries and Marriage and Family Therapy ... BA in Fine Arts/Humanities, Master's in fund raising, gallery/performance mgmt., PR, marketing, advertising & teaching.

Seel comments, "Would there be room for an ex-rabbi tentmaker here?" I would add, "Is there any room for God himself?"[1]

CHOOSE YOUR WEAPONS

There is nothing wrong with human excellence or education or training. But they are not the most important weapons in the battles we face as Christians. Paul writes in 2 Corinthians 10:3–4, "Though we live in the world, we do not wage war as the world does. The weapons we fight with are not the weapons of the world. On the contrary, they have divine power to demolish strongholds."

Paul tells us that we do not wage war as the world does. Actually, his statement is only half true. Paul and the other apostles did not wage war as the world does, but many evangelicals do it all the time. In fact, we are becoming highly skilled in worldly warfare—in the church and in many parachurch ministries.

How does the world wage war? One way that Paul mentions is with "the weapons of the world." Although weapons are only one part of a successful battle campaign, they are a very important part. If you want to defeat your enemy, you need superior firepower.

This fact was clearly evident in Operation Desert Storm. For days our entire country sat glued to the television as we watched America's superior weaponry bring a nation to its knees. Who could forget seeing laser-guided "smart bombs" strike targets with pinpoint accuracy and devastating results? Who didn't feel a surge of pride as F–15 Eagles, F–16 Falcons, and futuristic Stealth bombers roared down the runway and arched skyward for their next mission? The United States beat the pants off Iraq because of the most sophisticated weapons in the world.

In fact, if you are depending solely on worldly weapons to win your battles, it is essential that you have the biggest and the best. General Schwarzkopf knew this, and so did warriors in biblical times.

Imagine, for example, that you have been transported back in time three thousand years to the ancient battlefield in the Valley of Elah. Saul and the Israelites are camped on one side of the valley, and the Philistines on the other. Every day, the Philistines send forward their ultimate weapon, Goliath, to challenge anyone in Israel to hand-to-hand combat. And every day, Goliath taunts Saul's army, insulting and humiliating them.

Some vital statistics about Goliath can help us to appreciate why he was the ultimate weapon of his day. Goliath was over nine feet tall, which is more than a foot taller than the ceilings in most homes. His coat of armor weighed about 125 pounds. The point of his spear weighed about 15 pounds, and its shaft looked like a small flagpole. To top it all off, Goliath had been a powerful warrior ever since he was an overgrown kid. Perhaps you've heard the song about bad, bad Leroy Brown, who was badder than old King Kong and meaner than a junkyard dog. That would be a good description of Goliath!

Faced with that kind of challenge, how would you respond? If, like many Christians today, you take the what-you-see-is-what-you-get approach, then you would probably say, "We're not going to be beaten by a bunch of non-Christians! We'll find someone even bigger and stronger and meaner than Goliath. We'll run an ad in *Christianity Today*. We'll bring in the very best person money can buy. We'll offer him a fat salary, a benefits package, and a golden parachute. We'll show those uncircumcised Philistines!"

One thing you would *never* do is send a kid like David against Goliath. That would be like sending a biplane into combat against an F–16. David was young and inexperienced. He didn't even own a sword or spear, much less know how to use them. And when it came to size and strength, David probably didn't weigh much more than Goliath's armor, and David's head wouldn't have reached much higher than Goliath's belly button! Also, wouldn't you feel a bit silly sending a boy in sandals and a little white nightgown up against a warrior in full battle array? From a purely human standpoint, choosing David would be suicidal.

Yet whenever we look at life from a purely human standpoint, we function just like the non-Christian world, acting as though there is no God and the material world is all that exists. It is true that sending David out alone to face Goliath would have been a major military blunder, but David was not alone. When he finally faces the terrible Philistine giant, David denounces the what-you-see-is-what-you-get approach to warfare—spiritual or otherwise. He tells Goliath:

> You come against me with sword and spear and javelin, but I come against you in the name of the Lord Almighty, the God of the armies of Israel, whom you have defied. This day the Lord will hand you over to me ... and the whole world will know that there is a God in Israel. All those gathered here will know that it is not by sword or spear that the Lord saves; for the battle is the Lord's, and he will give all of you into our hands. (1 Sam. 17:45–47)

David reminds Goliath and us that it is not visible weapons, such as swords or spears or "Dallas men," that win the battles we face in life. The Lord himself is our ultimate weapon. He is the One who has the "divine power" we need to accomplish his will. Yet the only way that the invisible God will become visible to an unbelieving world or a faithless church is if we reject the what-you-see-is-what-you-get philosophy of ministry.

In order to reveal his power rather than ours, the Lord has often made choices and decisions that seem foolish from a worldly standpoint. Why would he send a boy up against a giant? Why would he tell Gideon to get rid of most of the men in his army before going into battle? And why in the world would Jesus have picked a bunch of uneducated, unsophisticated fishermen to be his apostles? He could have had the equivalent of Harvard MBAs, Fortune 500 executives, or megachurch pastors. Wouldn't they have been far better qualified to "get the job done"? Wouldn't their proven leadership and management skills have been a great asset in building a large, successful first-century church? The Lord's decisions defy logic until we realize that he wants to glorify himself, not his servants. He wants to demonstrate his power, not ours. And he wants to deploy spiritual weapons, not worldly ones.

THE SEARCH FOR SUPERPASTORS

Suppose that you are trying to find a highly qualified candidate to fill the position of senior pastor in your church. As you look over one résumé you notice the following report from the search committee:

> You asked us to be completely honest about the candidate's strengths and weaknesses, and we'll be glad to do so. He is an excellent writer and a respected author, but after listening to one of his sermons, we all agreed that he is a lousy public speaker. Also, those of us who had read his books were quite surprised when we met him in person. We expected him to have a commanding presence and to be confident and impressive. But we were shocked to discover that he is quite timid—although he is very nice and has a gentle personality. And

even though he must have some strengths other than writing, all he talked about during the interview were his weaknesses!

How would you respond to such a report? If you would toss that candidate's résumé into the reject pile, then you are in for a surprise. You have just rejected the apostle Paul as your senior pastor!

The "search committee" in this case was none other than the Corinthian church itself—or at least a group within the church. And when they compared Paul to their concept of an ideal pastor, he didn't measure up (see 2 Cor. 10:1–11). In fact, since Paul had left Corinth some other ministers had come to the church who seemed far more qualified than Paul. They seemed to have everything Paul lacked.

They were eloquent speakers who preached spellbinding messages. They were "big guns" who impressed the Corinthians with their commanding presence and outstanding abilities. These men had a bold, take-charge type of ministry that seemed highly effective. If Paul really was an apostle—and the Corinthians doubted that he was—then these new ministers were "superapostles."[2]

The situation in Corinth makes me think of a movie I saw a few years ago entitled *Twins*. The premise of the movie was that scientists had used genetic engineering to create the perfect male, played by Arnold Schwarzenegger, and with the "junk" left over they had created his twin, played by Danny Devito. The movie was a deliberate study in contrasts—tall versus short, strong versus weak, and handsome versus homely. Which movie character would best describe Paul? According to the Corinthians, he was sort of a first-century Danny Devito!

Although this conclusion may seem harsh (no offense, Danny), it seems to be confirmed by a description we have of Paul from early church history. A presbyter in the province of Asia during the second century described him as "a man small of stature, with a bald head and crooked legs, in a good state of body, with eyebrows meeting and nose somewhat hooked." Fortunately, he was also "full of friendliness; for now he appeared like a man, and now he had the face of an angel."[3]

Given the choice between a short, bald-headed, hook-nosed, timid, unimpressive person like Paul, and the tall, good-looking, eloquent "superapostles," whom would you choose to lead your church? If you say "Paul," then you're either a very mature Christian or you're not being completely honest! Most Christians I know would pick the superapostles in a heartbeat.

Secular studies have shown that a person's appearance and height can have a significant impact on their success in the workplace.[4] At the company where I work, the executives and managers are very gifted and capable people. But it is interesting to note that the president is 6'4" tall, the publisher is 6'3", the vice president of sales is 6'3", and the director of advertising is 6'6". Just like the Israelites of old, we want our "kings" and leaders to be like Saul—"a head taller than any of the others" (1 Sam. 10:23).

Yet Paul tells the Corinthians and us, "You are looking only on the surface of things" (2 Cor. 10:7). And when we choose our spiritual leaders because they are tall, attractive, eloquent, or impressive, we are following "the standards of this world" (v. 2). Worldly weapons may be effective in winning worldly battles, but they do not have the divine power we need to demolish *spiritual* strongholds.

How many Christian celebrities have to commit adultery or some other form of immorality before we hear what Paul is saying? How many more televangelists have to be convicted of fraud or mishandling of funds before we realize that perhaps we have elevated the wrong kinds of people to positions of Christian leadership? The outward qualities that impress people in the world may be great assets in business or politics, but they are not the traits God looks for in his servants.

The good news is that God often recruits wobbly warriors to fight his battles. Moses against Pharaoh, Gideon against the Midianites, David against Goliath, the apostles against the Roman Empire—these unlikely heroes became great because they trusted in a great God. In fact, when we call them heroes we miss the point. As Fee and Stuart have said, God is the true hero of every biblical narrative.[5]

THE SCRAWNY KID FROM ENGLAND

During D. L. Moody's first tour of England, an insignificant, beardless little man approached him at the close of a meeting and announced, "Ah'm 'Arry Moorhouse. Ah'll coom and preach for you in Chicago."[6] Moody was not impressed. Although Moorhouse was twenty-seven years old, he had a boyish appearance and looked about seventeen.

"Ah'm 'Arry Moorhouse," the little man repeated. "Ah'll preach for you in America. When d'you go 'ome?" Moody hid his disdain behind a veneer of politeness and told Moorhouse he didn't know when he would return to America. Inwardly he knew that he would not have told the man if he had known.

Moorhouse was a former pickpocket who had served time in jail before he was twenty-one. He was converted to Christ in a backstreet mission under the preaching of an ex-prizefighter and coal miner. After his conversion, Moorhouse had to wear thick gloves for a while to keep from picking pockets but later threw away both the gloves and his former way of life. He became a successful auctioneer, married his childhood sweetheart, and moved into a tiny home on the outskirts of Manchester. From that time on he devoted his life to preaching. As his reputation grew he became known as "the Boy Preacher." Even though Moody had heard of Moorhouse, he didn't believe such a scrawny kid could preach, so he promptly put him out of his mind.

Yet after Moody returned to America, an unexpected letter came one day with the irritating message that Harry Moorhouse had arrived in New York and would preach in Chicago if Moody wanted him to. Moody shot off a curt reply, "If you come West, call on me," but "thought [he] should hear no more about him."

He was wrong. A few weeks later another annoying letter came. Moorhouse was coming soon to Chicago and would like to preach. Again Moody responded in a brief and unencouraging way, "If you happen to come West, drop in on me," hoping that Moorhouse would get the hint that he wasn't wanted.

He didn't. He quickly wrote back, giving the date and time of his arrival. Exasperated, Moody realized that he would be in St. Louis on that day at the Missouri Christian Convention. He told his wife, Emma, that she should let Moorhouse stay in their home but gave strict instructions to the deacons, "Try him—and if he fails I will take him off your hands when I come back."

Emma Moody's brother, Fleming Revell, was the first to see Moorhouse when he arrived. Revell had expected

> some long-bearded, stately, dignified man—I went
> to the door and saw a little stripling standing there,
> an insignificant-looking little Englishman, he was.
>
> He said, "I am 'Arry Moorhouse."
>
> "What, sir?"
>
> "I am 'Arry Moorhouse. This is Mr. Moody's
> 'ouse, isn't it?"
>
> We asked him in and the little fellow toddled in.[7]

When the deacons met Moorhouse, they had strong reservations about letting him preach. But they decided to give him a trial run at a meeting where he could do little harm. They scheduled him to speak at a small, Thursday night meeting in the basement of the Illinois Street Church.

Yet as Moorhouse opened his Bible that night to preach, God showed everyone present that what you see is not always what you get. Although he "stood sway-

ing from one foot to another in his seeming awkward-
ness, you forgot all about it as you heard the message
coming from his lips."[8] One of those present that
evening wrote:

> We didn't quite know what to make of it. He
> talked differently from anybody we had ever heard.
> He seemed to have a different message from any-
> thing we had ever heard, and the deacons got their
> heads together just at the close of the meeting, and
> while the hymn was being sung, agreed that we
> would announce that 'Arry Moorhouse, as he called
> himself, would speak the next night.[9]

When Moody returned on Saturday, he asked his
wife how Moorhouse had done. "The people like him
very much," she replied, "although he preaches very
differently from you—he says that God *loves* sinners."
Up to that point in his preaching career, Moody had
taught that God hated sinners and their sin.

As the Sunday morning service began, Moody
noticed that for the first time people had brought their
Bibles with them to church. Although Moody had
always used a biblical "text" for his sermons, there was
little need for people to have their own Bibles open during the message.

With Moorhouse it was different. His primary text
that morning was John 3:16: "God so loved the world
that he gave his only begotten son, that whosoever
believeth in him should not perish but have everlasting
life." Yet as he explained the text he moved freely from
Genesis to Revelation, showing various passages,

people, and events in Scripture that revealed the depth of God's love for sinners.

Moorhouse's message struck Moody like a rock from a sling. At first Moody began to weep, but he later announced, "Mr. Moorhouse will speak every night this week. Everybody come. Tell your friends to come!"

Moody was never the same after his encounter with Moorhouse. Fleming Revell wrote: "D. L. Moody had great power before, but nothing like what he had after dear Harry Moorhouse came into our lives and changed the character of the teaching and preaching in the chapel."[10]

Those who look "only on the surface of things," who use "the standards of this world" to judge a person's potential impact on the church or the world, will never understand a Harry Moorhouse. Because people like him fight with invisible weapons, we sometimes assume that they have no weapons at all—or at least none of significance.

Yet think how different Moody's life might have been if Moorhouse had not been allowed to preach. For that matter, think how different biblical history might have been if David had not been allowed to fight Goliath or if a few ignorant fishermen had not been chosen as apostles or if a short, bald-headed Jew had not been turned loose on the Roman Empire.

As we will see in the following chapter, those who trust in worldly weapons may see worldly results, but they will never learn the truth of the statement, "'Not by might nor by power, but by my Spirit,' says the Lord Almighty."

5

Who Says Bigger Is Better?

I'll never forget my first visit to the Magic Kingdom at Disney World. My wife and I went there on our honeymoon, and we arrived at the well-manicured Disney properties on a warm, sunny day in May. When we reached the parking lot, smiling attendants directed our car—and a few thousand others—to the next available parking place, with smoothness and efficiency. Then a brightly colored tram glided to a stop and offered us a ride to the main entrance.

The real fun began inside. As we stepped onto Main Street, USA, Cinderella's Castle, the centerpiece of the park, rose magically and majestically before us, with its flag-topped turrets and pointed spires. Beyond that, signs showed the way to Tomorrowland, Adventureland, and Frontierland. Over the next few days, we saw and did it all—the Haunted House, Space Mountain, Pirates of the Caribbean, Twenty Thousand Leagues

Under the Sea. What a great place! No wonder they draw enormous crowds each year.

I had similar feelings the first time I visited a mega-church. As we drove onto the beautifully landscaped properties the mammoth "campus" rose up to dominate the horizon, looking far more impressive than any ordinary church. Once again, smiling attendants directed us and myriads of others into parking places. I fully expected a tram to arrive, but when it didn't we joined the flow of humanity walking toward the main entrance.

Once inside, signs showed us the way to various ministry opportunities—Promiseland, Son City, Sonlight Express, Prime Time. But that night, we had come to hear a special musical designed to draw in people from the surrounding community.

We took our seats in an enormous auditorium that held several thousand people. The focal point of the auditorium was not a pulpit but a large stage flanked by three-story windows with curtains that could be quietly drawn with the push of a button. Colored spotlights bathed the stage in a soft light, and a sound technician sat in the balcony above us at the biggest control panel I had ever seen. To top it all off, video monitors projected the action onstage to well-placed screens throughout the auditorium. This was high-tech stuff!

The musical itself was as good as any performance I had seen at Disney World. The singing was very professional, the acting was first-rate and funny, and the program was dazzling. In fact, I told the person who had invited us that this show was good enough to be on

Broadway, and she agreed. What a great place! No wonder they attract over fifteen thousand people each week.

I happen to know that this particular megachurch has an outstanding ministry both to the Christians and the "seekers" who attend there. Yet what often impresses people, and what makes many would-be megachurch pastors salivate, is not the values that drive the church, or the commitment to godly ministry, but the sheer size of the buildings, the huge number of people who attend each week, and the kind of high-quality productions we saw that night.

Most people in our culture automatically assume that bigger is better. And since this church is one of the biggest in the country, the inevitable conclusion is that it must be one of the best. Yet who says bigger is better? Does this notion really come from Scripture, or have we been infected by secular thinking and beliefs? If sheer size is a measure of success, then Disney World is far more successful than the megachurch I visited, because it has far more land, far larger buildings, and far better facilities.

And why do we have such a fascination with numbers, head counts, and attendance records? Is this really the way the Lord measures whether we or others have been successful in ministry? Frankly, if huge numbers are the measure of success, I think it is safe to say that Disney World draws far more Christians and non-Christians each year than any megachurch.

Even if we say that high-quality programs are a sign of success, Disney World would again win hands down. For pure entertainment value, who can beat Splash

Mountain, Star Tours, or a full-blown Disney parade? Perhaps Michael Eisner, the president of Disney, should start holding church-growth seminars!

Because our culture is so success driven, it is vitally important to know what kind of success God wants us to achieve in our lives and what other standards of success can get us off course. As we will see in this chapter, those caught up in the Superman syndrome often judge success by standards that are not only unbiblical but often the opposite of what we see in Scripture.

SECULAR RELIGION

A few years ago one well-known televangelist sent green prayer cloths to thousands of his viewers. God supposedly told him that the prayer cloth would be a point of contact, between him and the audience, for releasing God's blessing—with one essential condition. They needed to send lots of money with the prayer cloth, or as he put it, "Sow your very best seed." To those who returned the green cloth with some money, the televangelist promised great prosperity:

> SEND ME YOUR GREEN PRAYER CLOTH AS MY POINT OF CONTACT WITH YOU!... WHEN I TOUCH YOUR CLOTH ... IT WILL BE LIKE TOUCHING YOU! ... *When you touch this cloth, it will be like taking MY hand and touching me.* I want the anointing that God has put upon my life for miracles of finances and prosperity to come directly from my hand to yours.... *You can reign in life like a king![1]*

According to the televangelist, within months of sending in her prayer cloth, one woman received $286,000 in bonds and $65,000 in cash. Also, as a spiritual bonus, her husband was delivered from alcoholism.[2]

Most evangelicals I know do not accept the "health-and-wealth gospel" as biblical. In fact, they recognize that it is a bizarre combination of the gospel and the American Dream. Quentin Schultze, author of *Televangelism and American Culture*, writes:

> Televangelists offer their own personalized expressions of the gospel as adapted from and directed to American culture. To put it more strongly, the faith of some televangelists is more American than Christian, more popular than historic, more personal than collective, and more experiential than biblical. As a result, the faith they preach is highly affluent, selfish, and individualistic.... These three aspects of televangelism's faith system ... reflect the American Dream, whereby a self-motivated individual supposedly attains great affluence. They also reflect the impact of modernity on the church.[3]

Yet surprisingly, the same evangelicals who would reject health-and-wealth teaching as unbiblical will often embrace a similar and equally distorted version of Christianity—one that joins the gospel and the American concept of success.

What does this odd mixture look like? Perhaps the easiest way to answer that question is to look at Success 1994, an American road show that had forty-one stops in major cities during the year and included such successful people as Ronald Reagan, George Bush, Gerald Ford, Dick Cheney, Colin Powell, Norman Schwarzkoph, Tom Landry, Bart Starr, Roger Staubach, Mike Ditka, Marilyn Quayle, and Mrs. Norman Vincent Peale. The show also featured Mario Cuomo, Larry King, Willard Scott, Paul Harvey, the Rev. Robert Schuller, and Zig Ziglar. While not all of the speakers claimed to be Christians, most were openly vocal about the importance of their faith in Christ.

Time magazine described Success 1994 as "part revival meeting, *The Music Man* and medicine show and all uplift, with dialogue inspired by the Bible, *Poor Richard's Almanac*, Calvinism, common sense and Horatio Alger."[4] Zig Ziglar gave perhaps the clearest definition of success when he said it is "getting many of the things money can buy—and all the things money can't buy. Money can buy you a mattress, but you can't buy a good night's sleep."[5]

In a sense, the mattress and a good night's sleep are apt symbols for this Christianized version of success. The good night's sleep represents the traditional Christian values emphasized at the seminar, such as the importance of character, sexual purity, and making Jesus number one in your life. The mattress represents one of the many things that money can buy. Because apart from a few pardonable exceptions—such as missionaries or Mother Teresa—most successful Christians are expected to have not only mattresses but an ample supply of money for other things as well. Based on his fees for speaking at the Success seminars, Ziglar should have enough money for a mansion full of mattresses. He received $30,000 up front for each appearance, and that is less than half of what Reagan and Schwarzkopf collected. But Ziglar quipped with the audience, "Anyone who says he's not interested in money will lie about other things."[6]

Yet how do Christians engaged in not-for-profit enterprises, such as church or parachurch ministries, fit into this scheme of success? There a religious equivalent for money is used. The "bottom line" is measured not in terms of numbers of dollars but rather numbers of people. For many Christians a megachurch pastor is the spiritual equivalent of a millionaire!

Richard Reeves, author of the *Time* article, concluded that "Success 1994 is essentially a secular religion preached by believing Christians."[7]

OUR SECOND-RATE SAVIOR

Yet according to the standards of success many Christians embrace, Jesus himself would be a miserable failure. Although some health-and-wealth preachers have made lame attempts to show that Jesus was wealthy, virtually everyone admits that he had little money and few possessions.

Even when measured by the "success-equals-numbers" formula, Jesus had a low score. It is true that he often spoke to megachurch-sized crowds, such as those gathered at the feeding of the five thousand. But John tells us that at the height of Jesus' ministry "many of his disciples turned back and no longer followed him," because they were disillusioned with his teaching (John 6:66). The situation was so bad that Jesus even asked the Twelve, "You do not want to leave too, do you?" (v. 67). Yet when Jesus was later arrested in Jerusalem, the Twelve *did* leave him, running away to save their own skins. And the crowds that had welcomed him into the Holy City eventually joined with those who shouted for his crucifixion (John 19).

Unlike many Christians today, who consider the size of a ministry one of the most important measures of its success, Jesus had a very guarded attitude toward crowds and numbers. John tells us that while Jesus "was in Jerusalem at the Passover Feast, many people saw the miraculous signs he was doing and believed in his name. But Jesus would not entrust himself to them, for he knew all men" (John 2:23–24).

Again, after Jesus had fed the five thousand, John tells us that when "the people saw the miraculous sign that Jesus did, they began to say, 'Surely this is the Prophet who is to come into the world.' Jesus, knowing that they intended to come and make him king by force, withdrew again to a mountain by himself" (John 6:14–15).

Later those who had eaten the loaves and fish looked for Jesus and found him on the other side of the Sea of Galilee. Yet instead of rejoicing that a large crowd had surrounded him, Jesus confronted these "seekers" by questioning their motives: "I tell you the truth, you are looking for me, not because you saw miraculous signs but because you ate the loaves and had your fill" (v. 26).

Finally, in a series of statements that seem deliberately designed to shock and provoke his audience, Jesus tells these would-be disciples that they must eat his flesh and drink his blood in order to have eternal life (v. 53). To modern-day Christians who are well-versed in Scripture, these words have a strong spiritual meaning. But to most of the Jews who first heard this message, it sounded like cannibalism! No wonder they decided not to follow him. Rather than catering to crowds, Jesus seemed determined to drive away everyone who did not have a genuine passion and desire for eternal life. He didn't want a large following; he wanted committed disciples![8]

And for those who believe that large numbers are an automatic sign of success and God's blessing, Jesus warns, "Woe to you when all men speak well of you, for that is how their fathers treated the false prophets" (Luke 6:26).

In an article entitled "Unlikely American Hero," Joe Bayly writes:

> It isn't likely he could fill in at most seminars because he defined success in non-material terms.
>
> It isn't likely he could serve on the board of a Christian institution because he was poor.
>
> It isn't likely he could run an electronic church because he told a rich man to give away his money to the poor, not to support his own ministry.
>
> It isn't likely he could be a counselor because he reinforced people's sense of sin, was directive, and turned from those who didn't respond.

It isn't likely he'd be asked to supply many pulpits because he often just told stories. And they were short.

It isn't likely he'd be asked to teach at a seminary because he had no earned doctorate and spent most of his time in practical work with his students.

It isn't likely he could serve on a Christian college faculty because he drank wine.

It isn't likely his opinion would be sought or heeded because he spoke of his followers in terms of a "little flock" and "two or three," warned against times when all men speak well of believers, and said that they should expect to be persecuted.

It isn't likely he'd expect people to come into church buildings; he'd probably be preaching in Central Park or the Boston Commons.

...If Jesus were here today.

Poor Church, poor world.[9]

GREAT "FAILURES" IN CHURCH HISTORY

Church history is filled with great men and women who would be considered failures when measured by the success-equals-numbers formula. Two good examples come from modern missions.

The first is David Brainerd, who was born in Haddam, Connecticut, in 1718. During Brainerd's student days at Yale College, he heard a man named Ebenezer Pemberton give a passionate plea for missionaries to work among the Indians. Brainerd responded and in 1742 he was appointed to serve his first term in Kaunaumeek, New York.

He threw himself eagerly into the task, walking three miles each day through difficult terrain to preach the gospel to a nearby tribe. Yet in March 1744, after a year in Kaunaumeek, he didn't have even a single convert! He wrote, "My heart was sunk.... It seemed to me I should never have any success among the Indians."[10]

Discouraged but still determined, Brainerd moved to Pennsylvania, to the forks of the Delaware River. Although the Indians there received him warmly and even allowed him to preach in the chief's tent, progress was painfully slow. His Indian interpreter, Tattamy, had a drinking problem and did a poor job of translating Brainerd's sermons to his audience. By the end of his second year as a missionary, Brainerd's only converts were Tattamy and his wife.

In 1745 Brainerd moved eighty-five miles to the south, to Crossweeksung, New Jersey. There he finally saw some fruit for his labors. Revival broke out among the Indians, and by the spring of 1746 converts numbered nearly one hundred and fifty. Although Brainerd and the angels in heaven were thrilled, imagine how insignificant such numbers would seem to church-growth experts today. The rest rooms in some mega-churches have enough seats to hold that many people!

It would be nice to say that Brainerd went on to reach thousands of Indians for Christ, but he didn't. After the revival his health was broken. A woman named Jerusha, who was the daughter of the great preacher and scholar Jonathan Edwards, tried to nurse Brainerd back to health, but he died of consumption on October 9, 1747.

William Carey is another example of someone who failed at playing the numbers game. Carey was born on August 17, 1761, in the little village of Paulerspury, a rural community in England. He became a Christian when he was seventeen and later became the preacher of a tiny Baptist church in the town of Moulton. Although Carey sought ordination, the members of the ordination committee went to hear him preach and concluded that he wasn't ready—an opinion they held for another two years!

Finally, after he was ordained, Carey began to be dissatisfied with the hyper-Calvinism of his Baptist associates, who seemed to have little concern for world evangelization. When a Baptist association asked for topics for discussion, Carey proposed what at that time seemed like a bombshell: "Whether the command given to the apostles to teach all nations was not binding on all succeeding ministers to the end of the world."[11]

A fellow minister ridiculed Carey's proposal and responded with the infamous words, "Young man, sit down, sit down! You are an enthusiast. When God pleases to convert the heathen, he'll do it without consulting you or me." But Carey was determined not to be passive about the Great Commission. With the help of the Baptist Missionary Society, he set out for Calcutta, India, and arrived on November 11, 1793, with his wife and children and a fellow missionary named John Thomas. Carey's motto was "Expect great things! Attempt great things!"

Unfortunately, great things eluded him. In 1795, nearly two years after arriving in India, he did not have a single convert. To add to his misery, his five-year-old son Peter died from dysentery, and his wife, Dorothy, was so overwhelmed by grief that she lost her sanity and had delusions for the rest of her life.

Finally, in December 1800, after seven difficult years of missionary work in India, Carey was able to write home that his work had borne fruit—he had baptized a single Indian convert, Krishna Pal.

For the next twenty-one years Carey and his associates established nineteen mission stations throughout India and translated the entire Bible into Bengali, Oriya, Marathi, Hindi, Assamese, and Sanskrit, and parts of it into twenty-nine other languages and dialects.[12] He also cofounded Serampore College in 1818. But after all those years of labor in a country with millions of people, the entire mission team could claim only seven hundred Indian converts—fewer than those who go forward at a single Billy Graham crusade!

Yet we make a serious mistake when we judge Brainerd's, Carey's, or our own ministry solely in terms of numbers. Any vital ministry is a team effort, and its impact can only be evaluated over time. When Jesus preached in Samaria, he told his disciples, "The saying 'One sows and another reaps' is true. I sent you to reap what you have not worked for. Others have done the hard work, and you have reaped the benefits of their labor" (John 4:37–38).

Like Brainerd and Carey, sometimes we must work hard without seeing any results. At other times, we reap the benefits of other people's labor and see large numbers of people respond to our ministry. But when we look down on the sowers and put only the reapers on a pedestal, we fail to understand the nature of ministry. The success-equals-numbers formula is both unbiblical and unfair to God's faithful servants.

THE APPLAUSE OF HEAVEN

In a book entitled *The Applause of Heaven*, author Max Lucado describes the only fame, honor, and recognition that ultimately matter in life—the praise and glory of God. For me this fact was beautifully illustrated in a movie that won the Academy Award for best foreign film in 1987, *Babette's Feast*.

The movie describes a small religious sect, a devout group of people who live on the isolated and wind-blown coast of Denmark. The opening scene tells us that

> in this remote spot there once lived two sisters who were both past the first blush of youth. They had been christened Martina and Philippa, after Martin Luther and his friend Philip Melancthon. They spent all their time and almost all their small income on good works.

Most of the film is a flashback that describes why these women chose a life of obscurity, when the world had offered them so much more.

One day, for example, a young officer, who is a member of an elite corps known as the Hussars, comes to the village to visit his aunt. There he meets and falls in love with one of the sisters. She is radiantly beautiful, and he hopes to marry her and take her back with him to the world he wants to conquer. Her beauty would grace the courts and palaces of Europe, and other men would be filled with envy. Yet gradually he realizes that the dream he hopes for is impossible. She will never leave those she has devoted her life to serve.

Through a sheer act of his will, he represses his despondency and chooses the opposite path. Later he tells a friend, "I will forget what happened on the Jutland coast. From now on I shall look forward, not backward. I will think of nothing but my career, and some day I will cut a brilliant figure in the world of prestige."

A year later an even more distinguished person arrives at the tiny village. He is a famous opera singer from Paris, who has been performing at the Royal Opera in Stockholm. While attending church on Sunday he hears the other sister singing at the front of the church. He is astonished at the purity and quality of her voice, and he realizes that she is a diva, a woman who could have all of Paris at her feet.

He offers to give her voice lessons and tells her, "You will be like a star in the heavens. No one ever sang as well as you will sing. You will be the only star. The others will fade out by themselves. The Emperor will come to hear you, and so will the modest seamstress. You have enough talent to distract the rich and to comfort the poor."

Yet to his great disappointment, she too decides to stay and serve God in the village. The voice that could have filled the Paris opera houses and inspired the crowned heads of Europe remains in obscurity, bringing music and joy to only the woman's family and a little group of friends.

The climax of the movie, however, centers around a woman named Babette, who flees to the village after her husband and children are killed in a battle in Paris. A letter from the opera singer introduces her to the sisters and informs them that "she can cook."

The sisters put her to work immediately, having her cook not only for them but also for the poor in the community. Yet they instruct her to follow their bland and tasteless recipes to the letter, and she does so faithfully for over fourteen years.

Then one day she receives a letter from a friend in Paris. He has purchased a lottery ticket for her each year, and she has finally won—ten thousand francs! The money gives Babette the opportunity to fulfill a dream. She asks the sisters if she can cook a "real French dinner" for the upcoming celebration in honor of the founder of the sect. Reluctantly the sisters agree.

Soon a boat arrives with a cage full of quail, a live sea turtle, bottles of fine wine and champagne, a bag of truffles, fresh fruits and vegetables, a large block of ice, and ingredients for the finest pastries. The sisters have never seen such exotic items, and they begin to wonder whether they have made a terrible mistake.

When the celebration begins and the faithful gather around the lavishly prepared table to eat Babette's feast, they are joined by a special guest. The young officer is now a famous general, and throughout the meal his educated palate informs those at the table that the food and wine are of astounding quality. As he raises the crystal wine glass to his lips he remarks, "Amazing! An amontillado! And the finest amontillado I have ever tasted!" When the soup is brought to the table, he turns to his aunt and says with pleasure, "This is quite definitely *real* turtle soup! And what a turtle soup!"

The next course is brought in on a silver tray, and as the general looks down at the dish on his plate, he laughs with delight, "But that's 'Blinis Demidoff'!" Then as he is served champagne he looks around in disbelief and exclaims, "And this most certainly is Veuve Clicquot 1860!" But when the main dish is served, the general is so overwhelmed that he tells the people at the table:

> One day in Paris after I had won a riding competition, my French fellow officers invited me out to dine at one of the finest restaurants, the Cafe Anglais. The chef, surprisingly enough, was a woman. We were served "Caille en Sarcophage," a dish of her own creation. General Gallifet, who was our host for the evening, explained that this woman, this head chef, had the ability to transform a dinner into a kind of love affair. A love affair that made no distinction between bodily appetite and spiritual appetite. General Gallifet said that in the past he had fought a duel for the love of a beautiful woman. But now there was no woman in Paris for whom he would shed his blood except for this chef. She was considered THE greatest culinary genius.
>
> What we are now eating is nothing less than "Caille en Sarcophage."

After dinner the two sisters tell Babette how much everyone enjoyed the dinner, and she admits,

"At one time I was the head chef at the Cafe Anglais."

"We will all remember this dinner when you are back in Paris," the sisters tell her.

"I'm not going back to Paris."

"You're not going back to Paris?"

"There's no one waiting for me there. They're all dead. And I have no money."

"No money?" the sisters ask in amazement. "But ... the ten thousand francs?"

"All spent."

"Ten thousand francs?"

"Dinner for twelve at the Cafe Anglais costs ten thousand francs," she informs them.

"But dear Babette, you should not have given all you owned for us!"

Babette smiles at the two sisters and says gently, "It was not just for you."

Although *Babette's Feast* is just a movie, it raises important questions that relate to our life and service in the world. Would it have been better if the beautiful sister had married the young officer and become a part of elite society, or if the other sister had become a celebrated diva who had all of Paris at her feet? And would it have been better if Babette herself had gone back to Paris to cook in a great restaurant rather than serving those in the little village on the coast of Denmark?

In each case it is undoubtedly true that the women would have brought greater glory to themselves. But we cannot say that they would have brought greater glory to God. For in the end our success or failure before him depends not on the size of our audience but rather on the motives of our heart.

At the conclusion of the film, one of the sisters embraces Babette and says, "This is not the end, Babette. I'm certain it is not. In paradise you will be the great artist God meant you to be. Ah, how you will delight the angels!"

6

THE POWER OF PLAINNESS

During the late sixties and early seventies, Daytona Beach and Fort Lauderdale, Florida, were *the* places to go for spring break. Every year, thousands of students from all over the country swarmed the beaches for sun, suds, and sin. They cruised up and down the strip in their convertibles, honking and making catcalls to those passing by. They leaned over hotel balconies, leering at people on the street below. For an entire week, they cranked up the volume on their radios, blasted rock music through giant amplifiers, and partied through the night, with beer cans surgically attached to their right hands. Then instead of sleeping it all off, they laid out on the beach by day, exhausted and bored.

Like angels approaching a coed Sodom and Gomorrah, hundreds of Christian students also descended on these two towns to engage in "beach evangelism," also affectionately known as "cold-turkey" evangelism. In theory, the idea was to walk up to some non-Christians and share the gospel with them. (Sounds simple, doesn't it?) But in reality it had about as much appeal as climbing into a kamikaze plane and crashing into the side of a battleship. We dutifully volunteered for the mission, but we weren't too happy about it!

In fact, most of us were downright terrified. I mean, it's one thing to walk up to a total stranger and say, "Hey buddy, want a brewski?" But during spring break it seemed a little out of place to ask a group of belching fraternity guys, "Would you like to have a nice little chat about spiritual things?"

During our beach evangelism "boot camp," we felt somewhat relieved when our leaders told us an opening line to use in our gospel presentation. We were supposed to say, "Hi! I'm with a group of college students here on the beach. We're interested in finding out what people think about Jesus Christ. Would you mind if we asked you some questions?" The leaders assured us that it worked *most* of the time, and we loaded up our pockets with gospel tracts and headed for the front lines.

One of my friends, who was even more nervous than I was (he registered 8.2 on the Richter scale, while my trembling was about a 7.5), spied the enemy at fifty yards. There were five college guys sitting on beach towels, drinking beer and swapping stories. But before going in for the "kill," he decided to practice his opening line. "Hi! I'm with a group of college students here on the beach. ..." Then with more enthusiasm, "*Hi!* I'm with a group of college students here on the beach. ..." (*No, that sounded too enthusiastic,* he thought to himself.

Try to be more laid back.) "Hi. I'm with a group of college students here on the beach. . . ."

He paced back and forth like this for about ten minutes, muttering to himself. Then finally, when he thought he had it just right, he screwed up his courage, walked up to the students, and blurted out, "Hi! I'm a group of college students here on the beach."

They looked at him like he was some kind of nut, and of course he felt utterly embarrassed and humiliated, but somehow they ended up talking for quite a while about the gospel.

CRACKED-POT EVANGELISTS

In her book *Out of the Saltshaker,* Becky Pippert writes, "Christians and non-Christians have one thing in common: they're both uptight about evangelism!"[1] I believe that one reason we're so "uptight" or nervous is that most evangelists we know about are people like Billy Graham, Luis Palau, and Leighton Ford. They preach powerful gospel messages before enormous crowds, with astonishing success. We know that we don't have their extraordinary gifts, so we decide that evangelism is best left for the "professionals." We might pray for our non-Christian friends or even invite them to a local crusade, but we feel totally unequipped to talk with them face-to-face about Jesus Christ.

Yet as is often the case with the Superman syndrome, we have our focus on the wrong place. The greatest evangelist of all time tells us that "we have this treasure in jars of clay to show that this all-surpassing power is from God and not from us" (2 Cor. 4:7).

Using vivid imagery, Paul describes himself and every other Christian as plain pottery jars of the type that were common in the first century. When people look at the jars, they see nothing spectacular, attractive, or beautiful. After all, we're made of clay, not porcelain, and we're only jars, not Ming vases. If we were porcelain, with beautiful hand-painted designs and exotic shapes, then people might be tempted to focus on us rather than the gospel.

Yet the irony is that our plainness does not detract from the good news or discredit it but rather *enhances* the message within us. If you walked up to someone and offered him thousands of gold coins, hundreds of brilliant diamonds, rubies, and sapphires, would he really care what the container looked like? If anything, the plainness of the container would cause him to fix his gaze where it properly belonged—on the beauty and great value of the treasure. In the same way, because God has entrusted the gospel to "cracked pots" (as one person has put it), those who receive it realize "that this all-surpassing power is from God and not from us."

To put it another way, when we keep looking at ourselves and our own lack of eloquence or training, we fail to grasp the fact that "we do not preach ourselves, but Jesus Christ as Lord" (2 Cor. 4:5). God wants us to get our focus off ourselves and onto Jesus Christ.

Paul faced the reality of his own plainness and the gospel's power every day of his life. We might imagine him preaching eloquent, polished sermons to enthusiastic crowds, but nothing could be farther from the truth. In 1 Corinthians 2:1–5 he writes:

When I came to you, brothers, I did not come with eloquence or superior wisdom as I proclaimed to you the testimony about God. For I resolved to know nothing while I was with you except Jesus Christ and him crucified. I came to you in weakness and fear, and with much trembling. My message and my preaching were not with wise and persuasive words, but with a demonstration of the Spirit's power, so that your faith might not rest on men's wisdom, but on God's power.

Being rather chickenhearted myself, the first thing I notice in these verses is that Paul was just as scared as my friend and I were that day on the beach. Have you ever noticed that fear strikes at the very place where you want to appear calm? If you are afraid of speaking in public, it will probably cause your voice to tremble. If you are nervous about playing the piano, your hands will probably shake. And if you have to stand in front of a large group, your knees will begin to knock. Even the great apostle Paul was not immune to this pitiful fact about the human condition. Although he does not tell us what parts of his body were shaking, the Greek indicates a violent trembling that probably made him seem like a quivering, jellyfish evangelist.

If that happened to me, I would probably be so humiliated that I would say, "I *knew* I wasn't cut out for evangelism! I blew it so badly that they will never believe in Jesus Christ now." Yet the surprising thing is that the Corinthians *did* believe in Christ in spite of Paul's weakness, fear, and trembling. And both they and Paul knew that their response must have been a result of

God's power, because Paul had no power of his own—
at least not that day!

One other thing stands out to me in these verses.
Paul seems to be saying that it is possible for people's
faith to rest on human wisdom, eloquence, and persua-
siveness rather than on God's power. In other words,
what we often consider to be good and essential, Paul
views as a danger. We feel that an effective evangelist
must be strong, eloquent, persuasive, and poised. Not
willing to leave anything to chance, we want not only
the message but also the messenger to be as attractive as
possible. So we often tell all the cracked pots to get off-
stage so that the Ming vase can perform. Yet by trusting
in human power, we may get merely human results.
People may temporarily be swayed by the "magic of the
moment," but they have been impressed, not converted,
and like the seed that falls on shallow soil, their new-
found "faith" will not last.

FEET OF CLAY

Most of the great evangelists, those whom God has used
in a remarkable way, would be the first to admit that
they have feet of clay. One notable example is D. L.
Moody, who was born in a white frame cottage in
Northfield, Massachusetts, on February 5, 1837. Moody
had only a basic education, and throughout his life his
spelling was atrocious and his language was colloquial.

When Moody became a Christian at the age of eighteen, he went before the pastor and deacons of Mount
Vernon Congregational Church in order to apply for

membership. The chairman of the deacon board asked him, "Mr. Moody, what has Christ done for us all—for you—which entitles Him to our love?" The man who would one day preach the gospel to thousands replied nervously, "I don't know. I think Christ has done a good deal for us. But I don't think of anything particular as I know of."[2] His membership was rejected, and it wasn't until a year later, in March 1856, that he finally passed the oral examination, and even then by a very slim margin.

Even after Moody's career as an evangelist began to grow in power and influence, people were forced to conclude that the effects of his ministry were far greater than the visible cause. For example, in 1875 Moody began a series of meetings in London, in the Agricultural Hall. Attendance rose steadily, until each evening an estimated twenty thousand people came to hear the gospel. At first, some of the local papers criticized Moody ruthlessly:

> "There must have been thousands in that crowd of uplifted faces who looked with horror and shame on the illiterate preacher making little better than a travesty of all they held sacred." Moody's accent was called "broadly and vulgarly American." The word *vulgar* was worked hard in the London press, to deride Moody's accent and his preaching. The *Saturday Review* decided, from afar, that he was "a ranter of the most vulgar type," whose mission appeared to be "to degrade religion to the level of the 'penny gaff,' an itinerant gutter show like 'Punch and Judy.'"[3]

Yet in spite of the criticism, thousands continued to come to the meetings night after night, including the lord chancellor of England and William Gladstone, the former prime minister. One dignitary who was reluctant to attend was the aged Lord Shaftesbury. He had mixed feelings about the reports he heard about Moody, but he could not deny that God seemed to be working through this simple man. Finally, on Good Friday, Shaftesbury decided that he would go hear Moody and form his own conclusions.

The first thing that struck him was the plainness of the clay pot on the platform. He wrote in his diary that Moody's voice was "bad and ill managed," and Shaftesbury was a little scandalized that the evangelist's stories were "oftentimes bordering on the 'humorous,' almost to the extent of provoking a laugh!" (Remember, this was Victorian England.) Yet the fact that Moody was simple and uneducated forced Shaftesbury to conclude, "The Holy Spirit can work out of feeble materials." He went on to say that "workpeople, shopkeepers, merchants and lawyers, clergy and laity alike confess the power and cannot explain it. . . . It is impossible now to regard the power and influence as not superhuman."[4]

The fact that "we have this treasure in jars of clay" was clearly evident throughout Moody's ministry. On another occasion a Dr. Dale, of Carr's Lane Congregational Church in Birmingham, felt completely puzzled during Moody's meetings as the good news of Jesus Christ captivated the crowds, people

> of all sorts, young and old, rich and poor, keen
> tradesmen, manufacturers and merchants and young

ladies who had just left school, rough boys who knew more about dogs and pigeons than about books, and cultivated women—I could not understand it.

Giving Moody a sort of backhanded compliment, he said to him, "The work is most plainly of God, for I can see no relation between yourself and what you have done." Moody laughed and replied, "I should be very sorry if it were otherwise."[5]

BEHIND EVERY GREAT EVANGELIST

When we think that evangelism should be left to the professionals, we also fail to answer one vital question—who led these leaders to Christ? More often than not, their spiritual parents were very ordinary people who believed that God could use them in extraordinary ways.

For example, Charles Spurgeon, the great Baptist preacher who spoke to thousands every week during his lifetime, came to Christ under the influence of a person so ordinary that he was almost comical.

While he was still in his teens Spurgeon was walking to church when a snowstorm forced him to turn aside into a small Primitive Methodist chapel. He was a little reluctant to go inside, because he had heard that Primitive Methodists sang so loudly that it made your head ache, but his desire to hear the gospel overcame his sense of propriety.

Stepping into the little church, he noticed that twelve to fifteen people were present, but the preacher was notably absent, detained perhaps because of the severity of the storm. After several awkward minutes had passed, a very thin man, who looked like a shoemaker or tailor, took it upon himself to deliver the morning's message. He went to the podium, opened his Bible, and selected the text "Look unto Me, and be ye saved, all the ends of the earth."

According to Spurgeon, the man was so poorly educated that he couldn't even pronounce the words correctly, but he did his best to reveal the treasure of the gospel:

> My dear friends, this is a very simple text indeed. It says, "Look." Now lookin' don't take a great deal of pain. It ain't liftin' your foot or your finger; it is just, "Look." Well, a man needn't go to College to learn to look. You may be the biggest fool, and yet you can look. A man neen't be worth a thousand a year to be able to look. Anyone can look; even a child can look.

> But then the text says, "Look unto *Me*." ... I am sweatin' great drops of blood. Look unto Me; I am hangin' on the cross. Look unto Me; I am dead and buried. Look unto Me; I rise again. Look unto Me; I ascend to Heaven. Look unto Me; I am sittin' at the Father's right hand. O poor sinner, look unto Me![6]

The man went on like this for about ten minutes and then reached the end of his rope. Feeling a bit flustered, he looked around the room and noticed that a stranger was present, possibly the very sinner the man needed to drive his message home. Fixing his gaze on Spurgeon, he said, "Young man, you look very miserable." "Well, I did," Spurgeon admitted later, "but I had not been accustomed to having remarks made from the pulpit on my personal appearance before." The man continued, "And you always will be miserable—miserable in life, and miserable in death—if you don't obey my text; but if you obey now, this moment, you will be saved." Then the man lifted up his hands and shouted in typical Primitive Methodist fashion, "Young man, look to Jesus Christ. Look! Look! Look! You have nothin' to do but to look and live."

Spurgeon confessed,

> I know not what else he said—I did not take much notice of it—I was so possessed with that one thought. Like as when the brazen serpent was lifted up, the people only looked and were healed, so it was with me. I had been waiting to do fifty things, but when I heard that word, "Look!" what a charming word it seemed to me! Oh! I looked until I could almost have looked my eyes away. There and then the cloud was gone, the darkness had rolled away, and at that moment I saw the sun; and I could have risen that instant and sung with the most enthusiastic of them, of the precious blood of Christ, and the simple faith which looks alone to him.[7]

D. L. Moody was also led to the Lord by a plain and simple man named Edward Kimball, who was a salesman in McGilvray's dry-goods store during the week and taught Sunday school on the Lord's Day.

On April 21, 1855, Kimball decided to visit Moody to speak to him about Christ. At that time Moody was working as a clerk in his uncle's shoe store. On the way to the store, Kimball began to have doubts about speaking to Moody during business hours. He worried that the other clerks might make fun of Moody and ask whether Kimball was trying to make a good boy out of him. Kimball says, "While I was pondering over it all, I passed the store without noticing it. Then, when I found I had gone by the door, I determined to make a dash for it and have it over at once."[8]

He found Moody in the back, wrapping shoes in paper and putting them on shelves. Later neither man could recall the exact words of the conversation, and Kimball thought he made a very weak gospel presentation. Yet "it seemed that the young man was just ready for the light that broke upon him, for there, at once, in the back of that shoe store in Boston, [Moody] gave himself and his life to Christ."[9]

Such accounts are more normal than exceptional. Hudson Taylor, the founder of the China Inland Mission, was converted while reading the story of a sick coalman "who believed his sins stopped him from reaching Christ, until some pious visitors read him the Bible verse: 'Who His own self bore our sins in His own body on the tree.' The coalman cried, 'Then it's done— my sins are gone!'"[10] Taylor was so struck by the story that he instantly repented and put his trust in Christ.

In more recent times Charles Colson, the founder and president of Prison Fellowship, experienced the new birth after a friend and client, Tom Phillips, invited

Colson to his home and told him bluntly about his need for Jesus Christ. Phillips was no great evangelist, but he opened C. S. Lewis's book *Mere Christianity* and began to read from a section about pride. As Colson wrote later, the words were like a torpedo that "hit me amidships." He told his host good night, but a few minutes later sat in Phillips' driveway, sobbing and praying to Christ over and over, "Take me."[11]

From the earliest days of Christianity, when a person such as Timothy was led to Christ under the influence of his grandmother, Lois, and his mother, Eunice (2 Tim. 1:5), God has often used ordinary people to pass the gospel from one generation to the next.

Consider your own conversion. Although you may have been brought to the Lord by a famous evangelist or missionary, chances are that you first heard the gospel through your parents, a family member, or a friend—simple clay pots who were willing to share with you the rich treasure they had found in Christ. God simply asks you to take what you have freely received and freely give it to others, trusting in the power of the message rather than the power of the messenger.

BACK ON THE BEACH

A few years after my first experience in cold-turkey evangelism, I was back on the beach again, this time not as a student but as a staff worker with InterVarsity Christian Fellowship. It's not that we thought cold-turkey evangelism was the best method for sharing our faith. On the contrary, InterVarsity stresses the importance of friendship evangelism—building friendships with non-Christians so that the gospel can be presented during the normal circumstances of life rather than through an evangelistic blitz during spring break.

Why then beach evangelism? We felt that if students could learn to overcome their fears and talk with total strangers for five days under the most difficult of circumstances, then sharing Christ with their friends back on campus would seem like a piece of cake. Also, the Lord is glad whenever and wherever the gospel is presented to those who are lost (Phil. 1:18).

This time our beach evangelism project was in Port Aransas, Texas, and even though nearly ten years had passed since my first spring break experience, the atmosphere was pretty much the same. As I walked onto the beach the first thing that caught my eye was two guys sitting on the top of a Winnebago with long cane poles. They had attached ice-cold cans of beer at the end of fishing lines, and they were dangling them in front of every bikini-clad beauty that bounced by. Occasionally one of the girls would play along by grabbing the beer can and giving a tug. Then with great excitement, the guys would rear back and "set the hooks," trying to reel in their catch. I had to give them credit for their creative approach, even though their catch usually got away and stole their bait in the process.

By this time I was supposed to be a seasoned veteran at beach evangelism, who could train the students who were with me. Yet in reality I was just as nervous as I had ever been. The only real difference the years had made in my "clay pot" was that now it had a little pot-belly! Yet just as I had heard many times that courage does not mean the absence of fear, so I also knew that faith did not mean the absence of nervousness. I truly believed that God could use me in spite of my "weakness, fear, and much trembling" if I would trust in his guidance and power.

The conversation I most remember was with a young guy about eighteen years old, who had blond, shoulder-length hair of the style that was common at the time. We used our standard opening line, "Hi, we're with a group of college students here on the beach . . . ," and he agreed to let us talk with him.

Rather than giving the entire gospel to him in one load, like some kind of evangelistic dump truck, I preferred to begin the conversation by asking him a few questions about his religious background and beliefs. I found out that although he had been raised as a Catholic, he had stopped going to church and wasn't even sure that God existed. "After all," he said, "if God does exist, I figure that he will try to contact me in some way to let me know he is there."

At first I didn't know quite how to respond to such a statement. But then the Holy Spirit brought to mind words that I knew would sound outrageous but were also absolutely true. I looked into the face of the young man and said, "He *is* trying to contact you—he sent me to tell you about Jesus Christ."

7

So You're a Toe!

s I left the warmth of the ski lodge and stepped out into the cold Colorado air the snow made a satisfying crunch under my boots. I strapped on my skis, adjusted the cable bindings, pulled down my new goggles with the interchangeable yellow and gray lenses, and stood up. So far, so good.

It was December 1966, and I was on a ski holiday with Young Life. This was our first day on the slopes, and like every Texan in Colorado, I couldn't wait to show the locals what a talented flatlander could do. A few weeks earlier I had watched the French skier Jean Claude Killy plummet down a mountain at eighty miles per hour during the Winter Olympics. He didn't just ski; he attacked the slopes, always pushing himself to the brink of disaster as he captured one medal after another in the Downhill and Giant Slalom. I decided then and there that he would be my role model.

Earlier that day, when I had gone to rent my first pair of skis, the man behind the counter had suggested some short wooden ones. That would never do for Jean Claude! Didn't the man have some long, fiberglass racing skis, I asked? I would be willing to pay a little extra. Assuming that I knew what I was doing, he went into the back and emerged a few minutes later with a sleek, flashy-looking pair. Now I was ready.

The Young Life leaders *insisted* that I take a ski lesson before making my first run. What they didn't realize, of course, was that I already knew how to water ski, and I figured that it must be pretty much the same as snow skiing. So when the instructor showed us how to "snowplow," I went through the motions, but I knew it was kid's stuff.

When my moment of impending triumph finally arrived, I didn't put my skis into a wedge shape as I'd been taught, nor did I intend to make lazy, S-shaped turns as most of the locals were doing. Like the Olympic athletes I'd seen at the starting gates on TV, I pointed my skis straight downhill and pushed off with my poles.

It took me about ten seconds to go from a dead standstill to thirty-five or forty miles per hour. The first thought that flashed through my mind was that snowskiing wasn't a *bit* like water skiing. If you wanted to stop with water skis, you just let go of the rope. But now there was no rope, and my only similarity to Jean Claude Killy was that I too was skiing on the brink of disaster!

Where she came from, I'll never know. But suddenly, about fifty yards downhill from my death-defying run, a woman skied across my path, totally unaware of the human projectile headed her way. Like a heat-seeking missile locked onto its target, I could not get her out of my sights. Then when I knew a collision was inevitable, I fell backward at the last minute and slammed into her. We tumbled together for several yards and landed in a tangle of arms, legs, and skis.

After we had got back on our feet and brushed all the snow off us, I was amazed to discover that she thought I was an advanced downhill skier making a practice run. *She* apologized to *me* for getting in my way. I started to tell her the truth, but the words that actually came out of my mouth were something like, "That's quite all right. It could happen to anyone."

Perhaps I was inspired by her comment. Who knows what thoughts go through the mind of a seventeen-year-old kid. But after I made it to the bottom of the mountain, I decided to make another run.

I skied much more cautiously and slowly this time, trying my best to follow a zigzag course to keep my speed down. And I did just fine until I came to a steep, narrow part of the course called "Little Joe." Then in spite of my best intentions, I began to accelerate. As I reached the thirty-five to forty-mile-per-hour mark I whooshed past the other skiers, and the trees on both sides of the course became a blur. When I blew by some kids in the Young Life group, I heard them yell, "Sit down! Sit down!"

Sit down? I thought to myself. *If I sit down on a steep, icy slope while going forty miles per hour, I'll get hurt for sure, but if I can just stay on my skis until I reach the bottom, maybe I'll be all right.*

Unfortunately, while these thoughts were going through my mind I came rushing toward a fork in the trail. I knew that one trail was for regular skiers and the other was for advanced, but in my present state of mind I couldn't remember which was which. At the last possible moment, I leaned hard to the right—and instantly knew that I had made the wrong decision. I bounced up and down over the first two or three moguls and then became airborne, tumbling wildly end over end.

Because I had old, cable bindings, neither ski came off, and the leverage of boot and ski was just too much. As I lay sprawled in the snow I lifted my head, looked down at my right boot, and saw that it was at a ninety-degree angle to the rest of my leg. Both bones above the boot had snapped straight through! Foolishly, I reached down and put the boot back in line with the rest of my leg and then waited for the ski patrol to rescue me.

During the next four months, I discovered how difficult it is to function with only one leg. They put me into a cast that went from the bottom of my foot to the top of my thigh. I had to learn to walk with crutches, which wasn't too bad on level surfaces, but my bedroom was on the second floor, and climbing stairs was always a precarious experience. Instead of my normal morning shower, I had to settle for sponge baths. Then at school I didn't have any free hands to carry my books, so other students had to help me. At night I never could get into a comfortable position in bed, and occasionally I would have the terrible experience that everyone who has ever worn a cast knows about—the itch that you cannot scratch!

When they finally removed the cast after three months, my right leg looked like something they had dug up from a cemetery, and it was only about as big around as my arm. I still had to walk on crutches for another month, and it took two full years of physical therapy to get my leg back to normal size. Needless to say, I didn't rush back out to the ski slopes. In fact, I haven't been downhill skiing since my accident, which was twenty-eight years ago!

THE BODY OF CHRIST

The experience of breaking a leg taught me a painful lesson about why each part of my body is vitally important. But it also gave me insight into Paul's metaphor about the body of Christ. In 1 Corinthians 12:14–20 Paul writes:

> Now the body is not made up of one part but of many. If the foot should say, "Because I am not a hand, I do not belong to the body," it would not for that reason cease to be part of the body. And if the ear should say, "Because I am not an eye, I do not belong to the body," it would not for that reason cease to be part of the body. If the whole body were an eye, where would the sense of hearing be? If the whole body were an ear, where would the sense of smell be? But in fact God has arranged the parts in the body, every one of them, just as he wanted them

to be. If they were all one part, where would the
body be? As it is, there are many parts, but one
body.

Paul makes these statements to those in the church
who either feel worthless or envious of others in the
body of Christ. As is typical with the Superman syndrome, these people have looked around the church and
have made mental judgments about their own value in
relation to other church members. They have decided
that people with certain spiritual gifts are more important than other people—including themselves—who
have different gifts. In fact, they have even concluded
that their own gifts, and the gifts of other poor souls
who are like them, are of no value at all!

As a result of these mental judgments, they have
divided the church into the "haves" and the "have-
nots." The haves in this case—those who are the important and valuable members of the body—include the
hands (v. 15) and the eyes (v. 16). The have-nots include
those miserable church members who are merely feet
(v. 15) or ears (v. 16).

Today many people in the church value another part
of the body even more highly than the hands and eyes.
They are *mouth* worshipers. They exalt those who are up
front and on the platform either preaching, teaching,
singing, or acting in drama sketches. Realizing, however, that not all mouths are created equal, they tend to
give special honor to those mouths who also have television, radio, or conference ministries or who can write
best-selling books.

When I was a young Christian, I wanted to be part of the "Royal and Holy Order of the Mouth" more than anything. I attended a Bible church in Dallas, Texas, called Believer's Chapel that was famous for its all-star cast of Bible expositors. Two men in particular, who seemed like Moses and Elijah in our midst, were S. Lewis Johnson, who was a professor at Dallas Theological Seminary, and Bill McRae, who was a recent graduate of that venerable institution.

When either of these men spoke, it seemed as though their faces shone, the mountains shook, the trumpets blasted, and our sermon notebooks were inscribed by the finger of God! They were like Ahithophel, the character in the Old Testament of whom it was said, "Now in those days the advice Ahithophel gave was like that of one who inquires of God" (2 Sam. 16:23).

To my young mind, it wasn't as though their gifts were the most important ones in the church; they seemed like the *only* gifts. They proclaimed the Word of God from the pulpit, and those in the "audience" faithfully took down every inspired word. What more did the church need? I made up my mind at that time that I too would go to seminary and become a "mighty mouth," known and respected throughout the Christian world.

Yet Paul reminds those of us who envy other people's gifts, or who don't feel we have anything to contribute, that we are suffering from spiritual myopia. He conjures up a grotesque image of a deformed body made up of only one large eye—like something out of a horror movie—and asks, "If the whole body were an eye, where would the sense of hearing be?" (v. 17). Then another scary character, similar to the hand in the Adams Family movies, enters the scene—only it is a severed ear, trying to live and function on its own. Again Paul asks, "If the whole body were an ear, where would the sense of smell be?" (v. 17).

Fortunately, God is not into creating horror-movie monsters such as disembodied mouths, creeping hands, or severed ears. He has created the church to be like a whole and healthy human body, with each essential part fulfilling its God-given role: "In fact God has arranged the parts in the body, every one of them, just as he wanted them to be" (v. 18).

Yet we don't have to look very far to see churches that ignore Paul's statements and suffer the consequences as a result. For example, there is another church in Texas that exalts "Bible teaching" to the exclusion of almost everything else. The pastor insists that the key to the Christian life is getting "Bible doctrine into the frontal lobe" of your brain. He mesmerizes his congregation with the mysteries of "the Greek" and "the Hebrew." He has even developed his own vocabulary, such as "rebound" and "the edification complex of the soul," which enables the congregation to know the difference between the uninitiated newcomers and the enlightened inner circle of regular attendees.

But deformed churches tend to produce distorted church members. In fact, when members of this particular church move to another city or when students from the church go to college, they often refuse to attend other churches, preferring to sit at home and listen to tapes of their pastor. After all, who needs fellowship, when our frontal lobes are being filled with Bible doctrine? Also, at least two seminaries I know of are very reluctant to accept members of that church into their degree programs, because the students are so cocky and confident that they have a monopoly on the truth.

PROUD, PUFFED-UP PARTS

Not everyone in the church feels like an ear, a foot, or a lowly toe. Some parts of the body have the opposite problem—they are so inflated with their own importance that they feel superior to the other parts of the body and relegate them to a status of insignificance. Paul turns his attention to this group in verses 21–26:

> The eye cannot say to the hand, "I don't need you!" And the head cannot say to the feet, "I don't need you!" On the contrary, those parts of the body that seem to be weaker are indispensable, and the parts that we think are less honorable we treat with special honor. And the parts that are unpresentable are treated with special modesty, while our presentable parts need no special treatment. But God has combined the members of the body and has given greater honor to the parts that lacked it, so that there should be no division in the body, but that its parts should have equal concern for each other. If one part suffers, every part suffers with it; if one part is honored, every part rejoices with it.

Paul's argument to these conceited, self-sufficient "eyes" and "heads" seems pretty lame at first. "Hey guys," he seems to be saying, "you really do need those weaker, less honorable parts of the body." Of course, after Paul's words had been filtered through their grid, they would *hear* him saying, "You really do need those geeks and nerds, those social misfits who could never cut it in your elite inner circle." But a closer look at Paul's statements reveals how clever and insightful his argument really is.

He knows that people like this—especially the macho types who have an overdose of testosterone—take great pride in their "unpresentable" parts and don't need anyone to convince them that these parts are "indispensable" or worthy of "special honor." Just listen to any locker-room conversation, and you will discover that such people not only treat their unpresentable parts with special honor but even boast about them. And if you ever want to bring a group of grown men to their knees, ask them to imagine what life would be like without these "unpresentable" parts, and they will recoil in horror!

Now that Paul has their undivided attention, he asks them to consider the fact that the body of Christ is just like their human body—although I'm sure Paul wouldn't want us to take the analogy too far. The body of Christ also has "weaker" parts that are indispensable, and "less honorable" parts that need to be treated with special honor. In fact, God wants *all* the parts of the body—from the head down to the toes—to have "equal concern for each other" (v. 25).

FAN-TOE-SY OR REALITY?

When I read Paul's statements, I must admit that they sound great in theory. Just imagine a church in which the janitor received just as much honor as the senior pastor, and the church secretary was given as much special treatment as the chairman of the board of elders or deacons. But do you really know of any churches that function this way? If your experience is like mine, then you realize that most churches have a very subtle but real caste system, not unlike the rest of society, in which people are ranked in descending order of importance and often treated accordingly.

So we are forced to ask, are Paul's words merely wishful thinking, or do they have any basis in reality? Or to put it another way, if you are a toe in the body of Christ, do you really have anything valuable to contribute, or must you spend the rest of your life wishing you were an eye, a hand, or a mouth?

From both Scripture and personal experience, I can honestly say that the toes and other "less honorable" members of the body of Christ have something extremely valuable to contribute. In fact, in many cases their contribution will be remembered long after the words of the "mouths" have been forgotten.

Think about the parts of the body we normally exalt—especially those who teach us the Word of God. If you happen to be fortunate enough to sit under the teaching of people like John Stott, Bill Hybels, Stuart Briscoe, or Max Lucado, then you are extremely fortunate. But if we are honest, most of us have to admit that our pastors and Sunday school teachers are not quite so eloquent or inspiring. In fact, one of the most embarrassing questions you can be asked is, "What did your pastor preach on last Sunday?" Nine times out of ten, most people don't have a clue!

I say this not to denigrate the role of pastors or teachers but merely to put it into perspective. Like all members of the body of Christ, those who preach or teach perform a valuable function. But when you think of the people who have had the greatest impact on your Christian life, those who have provided support, service, or comfort when you needed it most, many of them have probably never set foot on a platform or stood behind a pulpit. And even those with public ministries will often have their greatest impact in private.

THE LIFE AND DEATH OF JOE BAYLY

Throughout his life, Joe Bayly served the church in a variety of roles. He was a staff member to Ivy League schools for InterVarsity Christian Fellowship. Later he was the editor of *HIS* magazine, and the first director of InterVarsity Press. Eventually he came up through the ranks at David C. Cook Publishing Company and became its president. He was also the author of several books, including *The Gospel Blimp*, *The Last Thing We Talk About*, *Heaven*, and *Psalms of My Life*. But many people knew him best because of the monthly column he wrote for twenty-five years in *Eternity* magazine, called "Out of My Mind." In that column he functioned as an evangelical prophet who pointed out the ways we were wandering from Christ and called us to repent. In other words, Joe Bayly was a noted author, a respected business executive, a popular columnist, and even a powerful preacher.

When Joe died in July 1986, a memorial service was held at College Church in Wheaton, Illinois. Many of those who packed the church that day knew Joe personally and wanted to testify to the impact this man of God had on their lives. Of course he was acknowledged and greatly appreciated for the public role he had served in the body of Christ. But a surprising number of people who were present at the service remembered Joe for his private, behind-the-scenes ministry.

Some recalled his hospitality and the warmth they had felt while visiting with Joe and Mary Lou in their home. One friend remarked, "I loved being at the Bayly's—the mix of openness, honesty, the cackling humor, the seriousness—and the feeling of freedom and an inner warmth of time well spent."[1] Others remembered how he had visited them in the hospital when they were ill, counseled them during a crisis, encouraged them with a timely phone call, or given them financial support when they needed it.

This kind of heartfelt appreciation for Joe's less visible ministry should not surprise us. After all, Jesus himself told us, "You know that the rulers of the Gentiles lord it over them, and their high officials exercise authority over them. Not so with you. Instead, whoever wants to become great among you must be your servant, and whoever wants to be first must be your slave—just as the Son of Man did not come to be served, but to serve, and to give his life as a ransom for many" (Matt. 20:25–28).

In the world there is fierce competition to be first, and those who aspire to greatness will often try to claw their way to the top, no matter who they have to step on or push down in the process. Yet few reach their lofty goal, because there are simply too many others who have more drive, more ambition, better education and training, or greater gifts and talents.

But there is a delicious irony for those who reject the Superman syndrome. You will find almost no competition at the bottom! Almost no one wants to be a menial servant or a humble slave washing the filthy feet of the saints. So while others are clamoring to become lords or executives or even Christian celebrities, you can quietly walk off in the other direction, down the path to true greatness. You may not receive any public recognition or be asked to appear on talk shows or radio programs, but those whose feet you wash will remember you.

And in the end, you will receive the greatest honor and recognition of all: "Come, you who are blessed by my Father; take your inheritance, the kingdom prepared for you since the creation of the world. For I was hungry and you gave me something to eat, I was thirsty and you gave me something to drink, I was a stranger and you invited me in, I needed clothes and you clothed me, I was sick and you looked after me, I was in prison and you came to visit me.... I tell you the truth, whatever you did for one of the least of these brothers of mine, you did for me" (Matt. 25:34–40).

8

Lord, Please Use Someone Else!

When I was about sixteen years old, I went to Lake Dallas one day with a friend of mine named David Miller. He had a great idea: "Let's jump off the train trestle that goes across the lake!" Even though I am afraid of heights, I reluctantly agreed. (By now you should realize that I wasn't too bright as a kid!)

As we drove across the bridge that spans the lake the train trestle was on our right, and from that vantage point it didn't look too scary. We parked the car near the trestle, put on our suits, and started toward our makeshift high-diving board. We walked between the tracks, stepping carefully on each railroad tie, heading for the middle of the lake, where it would be deep enough to jump off.

When we finally reached a good spot, we inched our way toward the edge and looked down. Immediately my heart started pounding. It may have looked safe from a distance, but we were over thirty feet above the water—about the height of a three-story building. I scooted back a few inches, trying not to look terrified. David did the same.

Neither one of us spoke for the first few minutes. We just stared down at the abyss, trying to decide what to do. Finally I broke the awkward silence and said, "Why don't you go first." I figured that David could be our guinea pig and that if he survived the jump, I would have a better idea about the real dangers of the situation. (I wasn't *totally* stupid.)

But instead he made a shrewd countermove. "That's OK. *You* go first, and then I'll follow you."

"No way!" I said with determination. "You go first, and I'll follow you." We were clearly at an impasse, so we scooted back a few more inches and sat there trying to get up enough courage to jump.

After about thirty seemingly endless minutes, David finally said, "I'm going to do it!" And before I could even reply, he stood up, walked toward the edge, and jumped off. I watched his descent with both fear and admiration and heard him hit the water with a loud splash. Almost immediately he came back to the surface and, treading water, looked up at me excitedly and said, "It's *great!* You'll love it. Come on and jump."

There are times when you simply shut off your brain and put your body on autopilot. This was one of those times. I didn't think; I don't even remember jumping. But suddenly I felt a rush of adrenaline and the kind of thrill you experience on a roller-coaster ride when, after slowly clacking to the top of the highest hill, you plummet straight down, screaming and laughing with the others on the ride.

I'm sure that I wouldn't have scored very high in the Olympic diving competition, with my eyes half closed, my fists and teeth tightly clenched, and my feet and legs splayed outward. Also, I didn't hit the water with that professional "rip" that barely leaves a ripple on the surface. My thunderous splash would have soaked the judges. Still, it was a 10 for me, and like David, I came quickly to the surface and yelled, "That *was* great; let's go do it again!"

We swam back to shore and climbed excitedly up the steep hill that led to the trestle. Now that we had faced our fears and conquered them, we were confident that our second jump would be a piece of cake. But when we reached our original point of departure and looked down, a strange thing happened. David gulped, looked over at me, and said, "I went first last time. You jump first this time."

"I don't want to go first," I told him. "You go first again."

Then we began to repeat our previous ritual of sitting and staring silently down at the water, trying to muster enough courage to make a second plunge. We were at the lake for about two hours, and I think we managed to jump three times. Each jump was just as exciting as the one before, but for some reason, we always lost our courage when we reached the top and looked down, and we *always* tried to get each other to jump first.

Now that I am an adult, people seldom invite me to jump off train trestles. But I am frequently asked to do things that require a leap of faith. You would think that after years of facing my fears and conquering them by God's grace, such challenges would be a piece of cake. But unfortunately, I often respond in the same way I did that day at the lake: *"I don't want to do it!"*

I know my response is far from unique. After studying Scriptures and talking with numerous people, I have discovered that many biblical characters and many of my contemporaries feel just like I do. When asked to do something frightening—something that takes them out of their comfort zone into an area of risk—they reply, *"Lord, please use someone else!"*

In this chapter, we will look at one outstanding biblical character, Moses, who surprisingly demonstrates all of the fears and feelings of inadequacy many of us experience when faced with new challenges. In Exodus 3–4 God asks Moses to become his spokesman to Pharaoh and to lead Israel out of Egypt. By looking at each of Moses' objections to God, and the encouraging ways God responds to him, we can learn how to step out in faith when our courage fails us and we feel overwhelmed with weakness.

"WHO AM I?"

Moses' first response is, "Who am I, that I should go to Pharaoh and bring the Israelites out of Egypt?" (Ex. 3:11). At this point in his life, Moses was not exactly a corporate executive or a high-profile politician who was comfortable in the corridors of power. He had spent the last forty years of his life living in a tent, and his only "management" responsibilities had been tending the sheep of his father-in-law, Jethro. Why in the world would God select *him* to confront the most powerful ruler on the planet and to lead a nation of over a million people? And to top it all off, Moses was well past his prime. At eighty years old, he might have seemed better suited to lead a shuffleboard tournament at the local retirement village than to take on the enormous responsibility God offered him!

When the Baptist preacher Charles Spurgeon was only nineteen years old, he received a similar call. He was asked to leave his tiny village church in order to become pastor of one of the most prestigious churches in London, although in recent years the church had declined in membership. At first he was so shocked at the offer that he wrote back and asked if they had the right Spurgeon. When the pulpit committee assured him that they did, he reluctantly accepted the position on a six-month trial basis—a condition he imposed on himself.

Within a few months Park Street Church grew from less than two hundred to over a thousand people, and a temporary meeting site was arranged at Exter Hall so that the church could be enlarged. The new meeting place could seat four to five thousand, but at the first service it filled to capacity, and hundreds stood outside hoping to get in.

Finally, in desperation, the church rented the largest auditorium in London, the Surrey Gardens Music Hall, which had three balconies and seated over seven thousand. Yet by this time Spurgeon's fame had spread throughout London, and the crowds that came on Sunday quickly filled the Music Hall, and thousands more had to be turned away.

How did Spurgeon react to all this? In later life he confessed to some of his students:

> My success appalled me; and the thought of the career which it seemed to open up, so far from elating me, cast me into the lowest depth, out of which I uttered my *miserere* and found no room for a *gloria in excelsis*. Who was I that I should continue to lead so great a multitude? I would return to my village obscurity, or emigrate to America, and find a solitary nest in the backwoods, where I might be sufficient for the things which would be demanded of me.[1]

Spurgeon's statement not only echoes Moses' words "Who am I?" but also captures my own feelings perfectly. Whenever I feel fearful or overwhelmed by tasks that are beyond my abilities, I begin to fantasize about the "simple life." I imagine moving to a small town, attending a small church, and working at an easy job that will never stretch me beyond my limits. Although my fantasy may sound idyllic, it is really a desire to "be sufficient for the things which would be demanded of me."

Yet the living God *wants* to push us beyond our limits, to put us into situations where we must cling to him. Is it any wonder then that his assurance to Moses and to us is, "I will be with you"? In other words, God is telling us, "I *know* you are not sufficient for the task I am asking you to do. But that's no problem, because I am more than sufficient for any situation you will face. So instead of running away, you need to learn to rely on me."

"WHO ARE YOU?"

Moses' second question to God was, "Suppose I go to the Israelites and say to them, 'The God of your fathers has sent me to you,' and they ask me, 'What is his name?' Then what shall I tell them?" (Ex. 3:13). After asking, "Who am I?" Moses now wants to know, "*Who are you?*"

In my opinion, one of the best scenes in *Superman: The Movie* is when Superman first reveals his superpowers to the world. Lois Lane is dangling from a cable, high atop the Daily Planet building, screaming at the top of her lungs. Just as she begins her long fall to earth, Superman changes into his flashy red, yellow, and blue outfit and swoops up to catch her in midair. "Don't worry, Miss," he assures her, "I've got you."

"You've got me," she exclaims. "Who's got *you?*"

Just then the helicopter that has been perched on the edge of the building begins to fall straight toward them and the crowd below. But Superman merely grabs it with his one free arm and gently sets both it and Lois safely back on the landing pad. When he turns to leave, an astonished Lois stammers out the words, "*Who are you?*"

"A friend," Superman replies warmly, and as he flies straight up into the air with a sort of half twist Lois faints in a heap.

Although both Lois and Moses asked the same question—"Who are you?"—Lois really had an advantage. She had already seen Superman in action and knew not only that he could fly but also that he was superpowerful, supermuscular, and superhandsome. She had even seen Superman save her life. All Moses knew firsthand about God was that he could talk and set a bush on fire without letting it burn up. So naturally, before Moses entrusted his life and the lives of nearly a million Israelites into the hands of this mysterious divine being, he wanted to know a little more about him. And "What is your name?" seemed like a good place to begin.

As you probably know, a person's name in Near Eastern cultures represented the sum total of their character, person, and powers. So when Moses asked God about his name, he was really saying, "Tell me what you are really like."

God's answer, however, seems puzzling. Instead of rattling off a list of divine attributes, such as, "I am holy, just, good, all-powerful," and so on, he says, "I AM WHO I AM. This is what you are to say to the Israelites: 'I AM has sent me to you'" (v. 14). The Hebrew word translated as "I AM" is the same word used in God's earlier assurance to Moses in verse 12: "*I will* be with you." In other words, God reveals himself not only as the One who eternally exists but also as the One who is and always will be present with those who trust in him.

Although it may sound irreverent to ask this, it may help to verbalize what many of us wonder anyway: How can we know that God is telling the truth? What assurance do we have that he really will be with us when we need him most? A simple story may provide the best answer.

A man once fell off the edge of a high cliff. But at the last minute, he grabbed a small tree branch sticking out of the face of the cliff, and he held onto it for dear life. As his grip began to weaken he cried out, "Can anybody up there help me?"

"I will help you," a heavenly voice replied. "If you will let go of the branch, I will catch you."

The man thought about the offer for a minute and then cried out, "Can anybody *else* up there help me?"

We can read about God's promises, study them, and even memorize them. But even though these are important and vital disciplines, there is only one way to *know* the truth of his promises. We must let go of the branch or jump off the train trestle or step out in faith in whatever fearful or difficult situation we are facing. There's no way around it—and that's the rub for anyone who wants to walk with God. How did Abraham know that God would provide a sacrifice other than Isaac? Only by plunging the knife toward the heart of his only son. How did the Israelites know that God would cause the Jordan River to dry up when they crossed it? Only by walking into the murky waters.

Moses was beginning to learn *about* God, but he would only *know* the Lord's saving presence in the numerous experiences of faith that awaited him. And even though we may wish there were some other way for us, there isn't and never will be.

"BUT WHAT IF I FAIL?"

Moses' third response to the Lord has two parts that are closely related. "What if they do not believe me or listen to me and say, 'The LORD did not appear to you'?" (Ex. 4:1). Then a few verses later he says, "O Lord, I have never been eloquent, neither in the past nor since you have spoken to your servant. I am slow of speech and tongue" (v. 10).

I hope that I am not reading into the text, but as I look at Moses' statements what I really hear him saying to God is, "What if I *fail?* What if I go to the Israelites, making all these great claims about having spoken with you and about becoming their new leader, and they laugh in my face? Or to make matters even worse, what if I go to mighty Pharaoh in order to tell him what you have said, and I get tongue-tied and begin to stammer or stutter and make an utter fool of myself?"

The fear of failure and of being publicly humiliated is one of the most powerful obstacles to trusting God. For me this fear has been primarily focused on one area, although it affects many areas of my life.

About sixteen years ago when I was a staff worker with InterVarsity Christian Fellowship, I went to a camp in the Colorado Rockies. The first night I was there, the camp director gathered all of the staff together for a get-acquainted session. We sat in a circle inside a rustic log building, and he said to us, "Why don't we go around the circle and tell a little about ourselves?"

Up to this point, I had been talking and laughing with everyone else, but when the director made this statement, a wave of terror swept over me. At the time, I was going through one of the most difficult periods of my life, and I feared that if people found out about my struggles, I would be asked to resign. Although the director's request seemed simple enough, he was asking me to open a door in my heart that I had closed and double-bolted because of the skeletons behind the door. If I opened it even a little, I wondered, would people see more than I wanted them to see?

By the time my turn to "share" came up, I was paralyzed with fear. I opened my mouth to speak, but no words came out. Then I tried a second time and barely managed to squeak out a few statements, but my voice sounded like I had inhaled helium, and the volume was just above a whisper. Knowing that I couldn't go on, I said, "I have been going through a difficult time lately, although the Lord has been with me." I didn't say any more, but I felt completely and utterly humiliated.

That painful experience and others like them during that period of my life taught me that I cannot always be in control of my emotions or my body—sometimes they can seize control of me! That dark realization has made me want to avoid *any* fearful situation in which I might have a repeat performance of that night in Colorado. It affects me especially when I am asked to speak in front of a large group, even though I have spoken in group settings many times since then. I tend to imagine being introduced to the group and then becoming like a quivering jellyfish in front of them, unable to give my talk or sermon. And even though my fears have never got out of control in front of a group—at least not in a way that most people would notice—I still hesitate to accept speaking engagements, because (I say to myself) it *could* happen next time.

You should know, however, something that took me years to realize. For a long time I thought I was afraid of public speaking, and I kept wondering why that fear would not go away even when I spoke fairly regularly. Then it dawned on me gradually that, in the words of President Roosevelt, "We have nothing to fear but fear itself." I wasn't afraid of public speaking—at least, not more so than any other person. I was afraid of *losing control* because of my fear and becoming humiliated as a result. Public speaking is merely one situation in which that might happen.

I have also discovered that most people's fears are about losing control or facing situations over which they have no control. Some people fear being laid off at work, knowing that they are at the mercy of their employers. Others fear getting cancer, knowing that it could strike at any moment without warning. Still others fear that something will happen to their children or their spouse—again, situations over which they have no control.

Yet when you stop and think about it, because we are human and not superhuman, there are very few areas of life in which we have complete control. We can strive to be physically fit and still drop dead of a heart attack, as the famous runner Jim Fix did. We can spend a lifetime building financial security, as many did just before the great stock market crash in 1929, and still be wiped out overnight. We can be excellent employees at work, receive high job reviews each year, and still be the victims of corporate downsizing and restructuring.

When our limitations finally stare us in the face, we can have one of two responses. First, we can either try to avoid every situation we cannot control, which will make us withdraw from life and from everything that will challenge us or make us grow. Or we can let the Lord be God and realize that *he* is in control, and that he "holds in his hand our life and all our ways" (Dan. 5:23).

"LORD, PLEASE SEND SOMEONE ELSE!"

After the Lord answers every one of Moses' objections and after he promises Moses everything he needs, I think there must have been an awkward silence. As long as we have legitimate excuses, we can say no to our fears and still save face. But when every excuse has been stripped away, we either step out in faith or expose our cowardice.[2] Unfortunately, Moses chose the latter.

Moses said, "O Lord, please send someone else to do it."

> Then the LORD's anger burned against Moses and he said, "What about your brother, Aaron the Levite? I know he can speak well.... He will speak to the people for you, and it will be as if he were your mouth and as if you were God to him." (Ex. 3:13–16)

Like Moses, we sometimes simply refuse to believe God and to step out in faith—unless we can have some more "tangible" assistance. Because God is gracious, he may allow us to compromise and to take crutches we think we need, just as he did with Moses by providing Aaron.

A few years ago our pastor, Steve Armfield, called and asked me to team teach with him a class on spiritual gifts. Once again I felt the old familiar fear I experienced while standing at the top of the train trestle, looking down. But instead of turning to God in faith, asking him for the grace and strength to say yes, I started searching for crutches. "You'll be teaching the class with me?" I asked. I wanted the assurance that if anything went wrong, I could simply turn the podium over to him.

"Yes," he replied. "We'll do this together."

Then I asked an even more important question: "How *large* is the class?"

"I think it will be quite small," he said. "About twenty people. Most of the church will be attending another class that will be held at the same time as ours."

Twenty people, I thought to myself. *I can handle that.* So reluctantly I said yes.

When the morning of the first class arrived, I walked into the sanctuary where the class was being held, expecting to see a handful of people. But to my great surprise and horror, the place was packed—at least for one of our Sunday school classes. As I sat down beside the pastor he leaned over to me and said softly, "The other class was canceled, so everyone will be in here with us."

At that moment, I remember looking up to heaven and saying to God, "You *tricked* me!" But then I also had an overwhelming sense that if God had maneuvered me into this situation, he must know what he is doing.

He did. That class opened up a teaching ministry for me at our church, a ministry that has continued to this day. In the process, I have been stretched and have experienced great joy and affirmation as I use one of the gifts God has given me. And thankfully, a number of people in my classes have told me that they have been helped as well. But none of this would have happened if I had said, "Lord, please use someone else!" and walked away from God's gentle nudges.

Now, my little episode in Sunday school may seem like small potatoes to you, and in a sense it is. But I think it is representative of many situations—both large and small—we face each day, situations in which we can step out in faith or turn away in fear.

Think of all that Moses would have missed if he had refused God's call because of his own feelings of inadequacy. He never would have stretched out his staff and seen the Red Sea part before him and the Israelites. He never would have gone to the summit of Mount Sinai to receive the Ten Commandments. He never would have seen God's glory or talked with him face-to-face. And he would have remained a simple shepherd all of his life instead of becoming Israel's greatest leader and the author of the first five books of the Bible. When Moses stood at the crossroads that day, pleading with the Lord to use someone else, he had no idea of what he came so close to missing.

English essayist Sidney Smith once wrote, "A great deal of talent is lost in the world for want of a little courage. Every day sends to their graves obscure men whom timidity prevented from making a first effort;

who, if they could have been induced to begin, would in all probability have gone great lengths in the career of fame."[3]

As Christians, there is no shame in being obscure, if that is what God intends. Nor is there any honor in being famous, if we seek our own glory rather than God's. But there is shame and great loss when we refuse God's call, just as there is great honor when we seek to become all that he wants us to be in Christ.

In the book *Prince Caspian*, one of the Narnia Chronicles by C. S. Lewis, Aslan tells Lucy to follow him, but she disobeys. Later when the two of them are alone together, Lucy asks,

> "How could I—I couldn't have left the others and come up to you alone, how could I? Don't look at me like that … oh well, I suppose I *could*. Yes, and I wouldn't have been alone, I know, not if I was with you. But what would have been the good?"
>
> Aslan said nothing.
>
> "You mean," said Lucy rather faintly, "that it would have turned out all right—somehow? But how? Please Aslan! Am I not to know?"
>
> "To know what *would* have happened, child?" said Aslan. "No. Nobody is ever told that."
>
> "Oh dear," said Lucy.
>
> "But anyone can find out what *will* happen," said Aslan, "if they follow me."[4]

9

IT HURTS SO GOOD

In an article in *Runner's World,* Dr. Owen Anderson describes the first time he experienced "runner's high." On a summer night in Sioux City, Iowa, he and his brother left their home at around eleven o'clock and headed for a deserted athletic field.

They jogged slowly around the track for the first two laps and then picked up the pace. When they finished their first mile at 7 minutes, 25 seconds, Owen thought they were done, but his brother had other ideas. He grunted something about earning extra points on his "Ken Cooper aerobic-exercise schedule" and started a fifth lap around the track.

Owen struggled to keep up with him, but his lungs felt as if they would burst, his heart pounded inside his chest, and sweat ran down his body. After they had run three agonizing miles, the two of them collapsed onto the infield. The pain in Owen's legs and forehead became more intense and ominous each moment. Then suddenly everything changed:

> My body's agony turned into warm relaxation. The pain eased, and I felt more at peace than I had ever been before. I didn't realize it then, but I was experiencing my first of many "runner's highs."
>
> As you might expect, I ran regularly after that night. However, several years passed before I finally learned why I'd felt so good that night.[1]

What Dr. Anderson later discovered was that the brain produces its own pain-suppressing, mood-elevating drugs. "Because these substances act in the way that morphine does, they were given the name *endogenous morphines* (*endogenous* meaning 'created inside the body'). We now know them as endorphins—the drugs responsible for runner's high."[2]

This physical euphoria does not come, however, without a price. During the eighties a researcher named Edward Colt discovered that when well-trained athletes ran four to eight miles at a moderate pace, only forty-five percent of them felt better after the jog. But when they ran the same distance as fast as they could, they tripled their average endorphin levels. To put it into layman's terms: *No pain, no gain.*

I mention this article because it reminds me of a puzzling statement Paul makes in 2 Corinthians 12, the passage about his "thorn" that we looked at in chapter 3. There he tells us:

> That is why, for Christ's sake, I *delight* in weaknesses, in insults, in hardships, in persecutions, in

difficulties. For when I am weak, then I am strong.
(2 Cor. 12:10, emphasis mine)

The first time I read this verse, I assumed that Paul must have been some kind of spiritual masochist, a member of the first-century leather-and-chains crowd. My warped mind imagined that while he was being stoned by the angry mob in Lystra (Acts 14) Paul was pleading, "Oh, please, please, hit me again!" Perhaps his masochistic tendencies also explained why he and Silas sang hymns to God at midnight after being severely flogged and then thrown into a dark, cold, stinking dungeon in Philippi. I would have been groaning and feeling sorry for myself, not singing hymns. And if I had been one of the other prisoners, I would have told those two religious nuts to shut up so that I could get some sleep!

Please don't get me wrong. As I said in chapter 3, I realize that weaknesses, insults, hardships, persecutions, and difficulties enable us to experience God's power. And I have seen God's sufficient grace in the midst of my weakness on many occasions in my life. In that sense, I feel a kinship with Paul, knowing that both of us have had the same sustaining experiences, even though we are separated by nearly two thousand years.

But when Paul says that he "delights" in weaknesses, hardships, and difficulties, we part company. I don't delight in them; I *despise* them. I don't want these intruders spoiling the peace and tranquillity of my life. After all, what person in his or her right mind would *want* to be stoned or flogged or thrown into prison? Either Paul was "one sandwich short of a picnic," as they say, or he knew some secret that we need to discover.

Because Paul was an apostle and because his statements about delighting in weakness are part of Holy Scripture, I am willing to give him the benefit of the doubt. I assume that he was not really a masochist or a mental case but has something vitally important to teach us. So in this chapter, I want to wrestle with how we can go from despising weaknesses to delighting in them, and how the pain of running the Christian race can somehow bring us pleasure.

WHAT'S IN THE BOX?

In the book *Halftime,* author Bob Buford relates how he faced a midlife crisis a few years ago. A lot of us would like to have his kind of crisis! He was the president and CEO of a very successful cable TV company. He was a self-made millionaire, with a home in the city and one in the country. He had a happy marriage and a wonderful son. But in spite of all of his success, he wasn't fulfilled. In fact, he started asking himself some pretty serious questions, such as: "What is the center of my life and identity? What is my truest purpose? My life work? My destiny? What do I want to be remembered for?"

To resolve his midlife crisis, Bob Buford didn't go to his pastor or to a Christian counselor. He did what any hard-core businessman would do—he called in a strategic planning consultant. Not just any strategic planning consultant but a man named Mike Kami, who is one of the top people in his field. Bob describes Mike Kami in the following way:

He is brilliant. He is demanding. He is intuitive. He slices through all the pretense and posturing and hones in on the core. A top resource consultant for the American Management Association, Kami was, at one time, director of strategic planning for IBM, serving that company during its years of rapid growth. He was then hired away by Xerox for a seven-figure bonus to do the same thing for them. He is independent, iconoclastic, and ruthless in his analysis.[3]

Mike is also an atheist. But after listening to Bob talk for about two hours, Mike asked him a simple question: "What's in the box?" When Bob asked him to explain, Mike described an experience he had a few years earlier with the top executives of CocaCola. Mike met with these executives to try to find the *driving force* of the company, the primary passion that should motivate all of their decisions.

After a lengthy discussion, they decided that "great taste" was their main goal as a company. So they wrote those words down and put them in a box, and they used them to guide all of their strategic planning. Then a few months later when the company discovered a new formula that tasted better than the old Coke, they introduced "New Coke" and made one of the biggest mistakes in marketing history.

When the executives later asked Mike what went wrong, he said, "You must have written the wrong words in the box." So they met again for several hours and finally decided that "American tradition" was their true driving force. They realized that Coke was an American tradition, like baseball and apple pie, and that customers didn't want them to mess with their traditions! Now that the company had the right words in the box, they were able to make better strategic planning decisions, and they quickly recovered.

Then Mike turned to Bob and said, "I've been listening to you for a couple of hours, and I'm going to ask you what's in the box. For you, it is either money or Jesus Christ. If you can tell me which it is, I can tell you the strategic planning implications of that choice. If you can't tell me, you are going to oscillate between those two values and be confused."[4]

When I read about this incident, I realized that it might offer the key to understanding Paul. Why did he delight in weaknesses, while I despise them? Perhaps he and I had different words written in the box.

PAUL'S BURNING PASSION

We don't have to look very hard to discover Paul's burning passion in life. He states it in a clear and compelling way in Philippians 3:10–11:

> I want to know Christ and the power of his resurrection and the fellowship of sharing in his sufferings, becoming like him in his death, and so, somehow, to attain to the resurrection from the dead.

Because this statement gives us profound insight into the innermost desires of Paul's heart, it is worth exploring in greater detail.

I want to know Christ. When we ask whether someone *knows* Jesus Christ, we usually mean, "Is he a Christian?" But obviously Paul had something more in mind.
If I were to paraphrase his words in a way that better
communicates his meaning, I would write: "I want to
experience Christ."

Like Paul, I think that many Christians today have a
hunger to experience God. In fact, many of us were
attracted to Christ in the first place because we were told
that we would have a "personal relationship" with him.
Yet if we are honest, we must confess that it is very different from any other relationship we have ever known.

Psychologists tell us that strong relationships must
be built on communication. If that is true, then how can
we have a meaningful relationship with someone who
never responds audibly when we talk to him? Another
mark of intimacy is the ability to hold someone and to
feel their embrace. Children who are deprived of physical intimacy become withdrawn and aloof. But as God's
children, how can we feel the embrace of someone who
is invisible, whom we cannot see, hear, smell, taste, or
touch? Is it any wonder that so many Christians become
discouraged and disillusioned about their "personal"
relationship with the Lord?

Of course, all of these problems have been overcome
by the Incarnation. God has become flesh and blood,
someone we *can* see, hear, and even touch. As the apostle John says, "That which was from the beginning,
which we have heard, which we have seen with our
eyes, which we have looked at and our hands have
touched—this we proclaim concerning the Word of life"

(1 John 1:1). But now that Jesus has ascended into heaven, what do we do in the meantime while we await his return?

The problem has also been overcome in part by the church, which the Bible calls "the body of Christ." There is a very real sense in which Christ's love, compassion, and even touch are mediated to us through other members of his body. In other words, our normal distinction between horizontal relationships with other Christians and our vertical relationship with God does not hold true completely, because we do experience Christ through his body here on earth.

And, of course, the problem has been partially overcome by God's Word, which some have called his "love letter to the church." God speaks to us in the pages of Scripture and invites us to converse with him through prayer.

But I am convinced that when Paul says, "I want to know Christ," he means something more than what he experienced through the church or the Scriptures or prayer. He desires a daily intimacy with God's Spirit, a direct and personal experience of the only One who can satisfy our deepest longings. He is like the psalmist who wrote, "As the deer pants for streams of water, so my soul pants for you, O God. My soul thirsts for God, for the living God. When can I go and meet with God?" (Ps. 42:1–2).

I believe that this desire for intimacy with God is the primary force driving the charismatic movement. Although many people are initially attracted to the movement because of "signs and wonders," such as healing, tongues, and prophecy, I think they are really searching for something deeper. Charismatic churches offer people a God who "shows up" on Sunday mornings, who talks to them, touches them, and sometimes overwhelms them with a sense of his presence. I'm not saying that I think all charismatic phenomena are genuine manifestations of the Spirit. But if nothing else, the movement testifies to people's strong desire to experience God. That's what Paul wanted more than anything else in life.

And the power of his resurrection. Paul isn't thinking here about being raised from the dead, although he does mention his own resurrection later (v. 11). Neither is he thinking primarily of the power that raised Jesus from the dead. What Paul desires is to experience the power of the risen Christ in his daily life. In other words, Paul realizes that even though Jesus has ascended into heaven and we will not see him face-to-face until we go to be with him, his power is available to those who seek him.

We speak of Christ's power so often that we fail to feel the impact of what Paul is saying. Think for a minute, therefore, about one dramatic expression of God's power that we see regularly—the power of a thunderstorm.

My family and I were on vacation in Florida during what has been called "the storm of the century." This terrifying storm announced its arrival with the most brilliant light show I have ever seen. Lightning flashed like a strobe outside our windows, as though God were turning a celestial light switch on and off as fast as he could. Fierce winds whipped trees back and forth, snapped off branches, and made my in-laws' house utter an eerie moan. At the moment that I thought to myself, *Surely the worst must be over now*, an enormous explosion of thunder rattled the windows and reminded me of how fragile and helpless we were against such forces.

Scientists estimate that the power of a single lightning bolt in a thunderstorm generates as much energy as all of the power stations in the United States produce in an entire year. Yet if one lightning bolt is that powerful, what about the power of the entire storm? And if we cannot even begin to comprehend the powers of nature, no wonder we fail to grasp the meaning of "the power of his resurrection." The Lord who calmed the furious forces of a storm with the simple words "Quiet! Be still!" (Mark 4:39) wants to reveal his power in our lives. That's why Paul was so eager to experience that power and to see it at work in the lives of those around him!

And the fellowship of sharing in his sufferings. Here we come again to the puzzling part of Paul's desires. And here again Paul's desires begin to diverge from my own. I want to know Christ and to experience the power of his resurrection. But Paul doesn't stop there; he says that he also wants to participate in the *sufferings* of Christ.

Of course Paul knows that he cannot add anything to Christ's saving work on the cross. But there is a sense in which Paul's life imitated and even participated in the redemptive work of Christ. In 2 Corinthians 4:11–12 Paul writes, "For we who are alive are always being given over to death for Jesus' sake, so that his life may be revealed in our mortal body. So then, death is at work in us, but life is at work in you."

Just as Jesus died so that we might have life, so Paul died daily so that others might live. In other words, Paul had to go through intense sufferings, weaknesses, hardships, and difficulties—a sort of daily death—in order for others to experience the life-giving message of the gospel. And he not only willingly did so, he *wanted* to do it. Why?

I think Paul realized that his three main passions in life were a package deal. He didn't like suffering and weakness for their own sake, but he knew that they were an essential part of knowing Christ and experiencing the power of his resurrection. An Olympic athlete can *say* that he wants to break the world record for the mile, but his words are meaningless if he refuses the suffering and pain of Olympic training. In the same way, I can *say* that I want to experience Christ and the power of his resurrection, but my words are meaningless if I am unwilling to share in his sufferings.

I am not suggesting, of course, that we should actively seek to suffer for Christ's sake, as some of the early Christian martyrs did. That would be spiritual masochism. Nor am I saying that we should be passive about our weaknesses, doing nothing to remove them from our lives or from the lives of others. That would be spiritual fatalism. But in a fallen world, we will experience both suffering and weakness whether we want to or not, especially if we are faithful to Jesus Christ (see 2 Tim. 3:12).

Yet if we cannot escape from suffering and weakness, we *can* change the way we perceive them. We can even learn to delight in them—if we make Paul's passion our own.

OUT OF THE MOUTHS OF BABES

If most of us were asked the question, "What is your primary passion in life?" we would probably say something pious, like "knowing Jesus Christ," or "glorifying God." But if those who know us best were asked about our primary passion, they might give a very different answer, one that doesn't sound so pious. In fact, this happened to me recently.

A few days ago I took my young children, Katie and Chris, to the mall to do some shopping. On the way there, we starting talking about our favorite sports.

Now anyone who knows me well realizes that I have a passion for golf. As long as the weather in Michigan is above freezing, I like to play at least nine holes a week—and even more if possible. I subscribe to two golf magazines, watch golf on television, and even have a golf game on my computer that I enjoy playing.

But I get uncomfortable when my children think that golf is all I care about, so when the subject came up, I tried to give a more *balanced* impression of myself. I said, "Yes, I do like golf, but I also play tennis and jog and fish and do several other things."

Katie and Chris wouldn't buy it. Katie said, "Dad, you play tennis, but you *love* golf!" Then as we were walking into the mall, she started mocking me, saying, "Golf, golf, golf, golf, golf, golf, golf."

"No toys for you, young lady!" I said, trying to get her to be quiet. But she only smirked at me and kept repeating, "Golf, golf, golf, golf, golf."

When it comes to our true passion in life, our actions speak louder than our words. So we need to ask ourselves, "Based on our daily behavior, what is the *real* passion of our lives, and what should it be?"

For Paul it was clear. He had such an intense desire to know Christ's power that he welcomed and even *delighted* in anything that helped him reach that goal. Paul wasn't a masochist or a madman; he felt the pain of life's thorns just as much as we do and knew the humiliation of human weakness. But he also knew that Jesus met him in the midst of his weaknesses, surrounded him with sufficient grace, and embraced him with divine power.

Through numerous intimate and personal experiences, Paul realized what I am only beginning to discover—even a barren wasteland can seem like a beautiful garden if the One we love meets us there.

10

THE POWER OF TRANSPARENCY

For several months Pastor Ingqvist, the Lutheran pastor in Lake Wobegon, Minnesota, had been planning a trip with his wife, Judy, to the five-day Rural Lutheran Clergy Conference in Orlando, Florida. According to author Garrison Keillor, one purpose of the conference was "to allow Lutheran clergy from small towns to get someplace where they can let down their hair just a little bit. Most of them are pretty short-haired people, so it's not a *dramatic* thing." Keillor goes on to say:

> It's important to them once a year. Because if you live in a town of a thousand people, and you are a representative of the faith, your life is an open book to people. And some of the most interesting parts you want to write in a pretty small type, as faintly as possible, because people are reading you

all of the time and reading you *literally*. So that if you are sitting in your study and you turn and the corner of the desk catches your knee—that part that the doctor taps to find out if you're still alive—the choice of language that's open to you at that point is pretty narrow and doesn't include all the most satisfying stuff!

You're only human, of course, even though you're a minister. But if you stood up in the pulpit and *told* them that you were only human, their first thought would be that you had committed adultery, and their second would be with whom and for how long! So it ain't easy.[1]

Like Pastor Ingqvist, most of us find that it isn't easy being open and vulnerable, especially in a society caught up in the Superman syndrome, where everyone is supposed to project an image of having it all together. In fact, if you went into most churches on Sunday morning, you would never think that those gathered for worship had any problems at all. They look so nice and pretty and proper with their smiling faces and good-natured chatter in the narthex. Who would ever guess that Jim and Betty are thinking about divorce, Phyllis is clinically depressed and has frequent thoughts of suicide, Dave and Rhonda have a rebellious teenage son who is on drugs, Beth is struggling with being a single parent, Michael is addicted to pornography, and two of the deacons haven't spoken to each other in months!

If you think that I have exaggerated the situation for dramatic effect, just ask your pastor or local Christian counselor. They will probably tell you that the problems are far deeper and more widespread than I have described.

Then when given the opportunity to share prayer requests, either on Sunday morning or during a small-group meeting, what do people mention? You know the routine. "Please pray for my Aunt Minnie. She stubbed her big toe last week and is having a terrible time walking." "Please pray for my brother-in-law in Peoria. His hemorrhoids have been acting up, and he may need to go in for surgery." Or "Our dog, Muffin, was hit by a car, and the children are very upset. Please keep them in your prayers."

I'm not saying that these aren't legitimate requests. But many Christians share only on a superficial level and are unwilling to get beneath the surface where they really need help. As a result, they keep their image intact while inside they go from bad to worse.

In the Superman comics, Clark Kent was only a disguise, and the "mild-mannered reporter" was really the Man of Steel. In our case, the situation is reversed. We try to disguise ourselves as Superman, but beneath the surface, we are really only Clark Kent. Is it any wonder that we won't pull open the buttons on our shirt to let people see who we really are?

In this chapter, I want to explore this final facet of the Superman syndrome. We will look at why those who project an image of strength are most prone to spiritual weakness, while those who openly admit their weaknesses are able to receive the strength they need.

BACKDOOR BELIEVERS

In the book *Exit Interviews,* author William D. Hendricks estimates that fifty-three thousand people leave the church every week and never come back. To find out why, Hendricks interviewed dozens of these "dropouts" across the country. Although his interviews uncovered a variety of reasons for people's dissatisfaction with the church, one specific reason seemed to be prominent in several of the interviews: the lack of authenticity in most churches.

For example, a woman who is identified as Diana says that she left the church because people weren't allowed to express their humanity and weren't encouraged to be "real":

> I remember reading about Elizabeth O'Conner's church in Washington, D.C., called Church of the Saviour. It was so refreshing because it wasn't perfect. People were bumping into their humanity all over the place, trying to learn how to serve the community. To me, it was such a beautiful picture because it affirmed that we have a shadow; a dark, passionate, difficult side to deal with in our humanity. From what I've seen in the church, we never let that out of the bag.... Mainly, I guess, I want to have a church where people are more real.... If the church were more real and addressed people in a more real way, then that's the kind of church I'd like to be involved in.[2]

In another interview, a woman named Jennifer recalls that at a meeting of the church, she burst into tears and said: "Look, we're all coming to church and we're performing. We're putting on a big show. We're pretending every Sunday. I can't do this anymore!"[3]

In one of the final chapters of the book, Hendricks summarizes what he discovered about people's craving for "truth" and "reality." He writes:

> There seemed to be a feeling that religious situations too often lack authenticity. The truth is not told; people are not "real." Christian sermons, books, and conversations too often seemed to avoid the "bad stuff." Indeed, religion sometimes seems off in a world of its own. Yet my interviewees felt that if the faith is to make any difference in people's lives, it has to face cold, hard reality. It also has to get under the surface to a person's real self, to one's sin and pain and the things one wants to hide.[4]

Why do we want to hide our sins and weaknesses from others? Because telling the truth can be costly! As one person has said, "A reputation takes a lifetime to build, but it can be destroyed in a minute." We fear that if people found out about our struggles, they would no longer respect us. There is also the danger that we might be passed over for positions of leadership or that we might even be asked to "step down" from positions we already occupy. Also, people in the church are often notorious for not keeping confidences. Garrison Keillor claims that people in Lake Wobegon are afraid to be honest with their pastor lest they become an illustration in next week's sermon!

Yet even though it is costly to be honest, it is even more costly when we fail to tell the truth. In Ezekiel 13:10–11 the Lord rebukes the false prophets and says, "They lead my people astray, saying, 'Peace,' when there is no peace, and because, when a flimsy wall is built, they cover it with whitewash, therefore tell those who cover it with whitewash that it is going to fall."

Do you hear what the Lord is saying? It is much easier to cover a flimsy wall with paint than it is to fix it, so that's what we often do! We may have a flimsy moral life, but it is easier to cover it with a veneer of piety than it is to truly rebuild our life. We may have a flimsy marriage, but it is easier to cover it with a good coat of whitewash—which is a form of dishonesty and deceit—than it is to honestly admit our problems and reach out for help.

Ezekiel warns us that when we whitewash the flimsy walls in our lives, we may look good for a while and we may even be able to project an image of spirituality, but we face the terrible prospect that our whitewashed walls will come crashing to the ground. It is costly to be open and honest with each other, but it is even more costly when we hide the truth.

A FRIEND IN NEED

In 1977 a friend of mine who had recently graduated from seminary became an associate pastor of a church in Houston, Texas. My friend had been married for about five years, but his marriage had been very difficult, and it had taken a turn for the worse just before he accepted a call to the church. During his job interview with the leaders of the church, he struggled with whether he should tell them about the problems in his marriage, but he feared that they would not hire him if they knew the truth.

Shortly after he had been hired, he came to Houston to look for a place to live, and while he was there he stayed in the home of the pastor and his wife. One evening the three of them were discussing the fact that the church had recently gone through a terrible split, where half of the congregation had gone with the former copastor. The pastor said to my friend, "One of the worst parts of working with that copastor was that he was never fully honest with me. I think that if he had been honest, this might never have happened."

At that point, my friend felt about two inches tall and was overwhelmed with feelings of guilt. Slowly and reluctantly he confessed to the pastor that he and his wife were having serious marital problems.

Needless to say, the pastor wasn't exactly thrilled. He called an emergency session with one of the elders, and the two of them discussed what should be done. Finally they agreed that my friend could still come to the church if he and his wife would begin counseling sessions with the pastor, who worked full-time as a therapist and only part-time as pastor of the church.

Although it was a very painful experience, my friend was greatly relieved by their decision. His wife agreed to the counseling, and he began to have hope not only for his ministry but also for his marriage.

Seven months passed, and my friend's ministry was well received by the congregation. People liked his preaching, and the youth group he was in charge of seemed to have renewed enthusiasm. Although my friend's marriage was still very difficult, he felt that things would improve over time.

Then one evening the pastor asked him to come over to his home for what my friend thought was a routine job review. But after they had dispensed with the small talk, the pastor said to him, "I think you should begin looking for another job. Because of your marriage, you are totally unfit for pastoral ministry."

My friend felt like he had been hit by two blasts from a double-barreled shotgun. For many men, the two most important areas in their lives are their marriages and their careers. As he sat there in stunned silence, my friend saw both of these come crashing to the ground.

Then the pastor offered the following advice: "I think it would be best if you didn't tell anyone your *real* reason for leaving the church. This is a personal matter between you and your wife, and she would prefer that the matter be kept secret. After you find another job, you can simply announce to the church that you felt called into another ministry."

Like a sheep being led to the slaughter, my friend accepted this advice. Although he faced the greatest emotional crisis of his life and desperately needed the support of others, he didn't tell *anyone*—neither his parents nor his brother and sisters nor his friends nor anyone in the church. That was one of the greatest mistakes he ever made.

The second greatest mistake came a few weeks later. There arose an opportunity to work in a ministry to college students, and my friend decided to apply for the job. But first he went back to his pastor to ask for advice about the job application: "Shouldn't I tell the organization about my marital problems? After all, if I am unfit for pastoral ministry, how can I possibly minister to college students?"

"I would only tell them if they specifically ask you about it," the pastor replied. "You don't need to tell them more than they ask for. And since there aren't any married couples among the college students you will be working with, I don't see why you can't minister effectively in that kind of setting."

Again he accepted the pastor's advice, but it was a recipe for disaster. For the next four years of student ministry, my friend tried to appear "normal," while inside he felt as if he were dying. Also, he awoke each day with the fear that people would discover the terrible secret about his failing marriage and then ask him to resign, just as he had been asked to resign from the church. On the surface, his life and ministry appeared to be very successful, but no one knew the pain and anguish he felt. They didn't know because he refused to tell them.

When he finally came to the point where he could not go on any longer, help came in the form of a friend named Curtis Arnold. One day when the two of them were together at a student camp in Colorado, Curtis said to him, "We have been close friends for nearly four years, and I know you have been going through difficult times, but you've never told me what you are struggling with. If you know that I love you as a brother in Christ, why can't you trust me with your secret?"

"You're right," my friend said. "I should be able to trust you, and I desperately need your prayers and support." Then for the next two hours, beginning with the ministry at his former church, he told Curtis everything that had happened. As he poured out his heart my friend not only felt tremendous relief that his secret was finally out in the open but also felt loved, accepted, and renewed.

That was the beginning of his healing process—a gradual process that continues to this day. He eventually told his family and closest friends what had been happening, and he even decided to tell his supervisor. Although they were all greatly concerned about him and his wife, they didn't reject him as he had feared but rather offered him the help and support that he had needed all along.

I wish that I could report to you that my friend's marriage was eventually restored, but it wasn't. Although he did everything in his power to save the marriage, it finally ended in divorce in 1982. Yet throughout that difficult time, he was surrounded by Christian brothers and sisters who knew what he was going through and lovingly cared for him each step of the way.

I'm happy to say that my friend later remarried, and he and his wife recently celebrated their eleventh wedding anniversary. They have two beautiful children, and the Lord has graciously "restored the years that the locusts had eaten" (see Joel 2:25). Although my friend never reentered the pastorate, he has had an effective ministry in religious publishing, and by God's grace the books he has edited and written have reached far more people than he ever could have reached in his former church.

You may be wondering how I know so many of the details of this situation. I know because the "friend" I have been describing is me. I mention my story because it illustrates both the high cost of telling the truth and the much higher cost of keeping silent. I know from experience that we can only maintain a veneer of spirituality for so long. But if we want to experience true spiritual growth, we must follow James' command: "Confess your sins to each other and pray for each other so that you may be healed" (James 5:16).

WOUNDED HEALERS

In the book *The Wounded Healer,* author Henri Nouwen claims that only those who admit their own brokenness, both to themselves and to others, can ever be effective in ministry.[5] This is similar to what the author of Hebrews says about the high priests in the Old Testament:

> Every high priest is selected from among men and is appointed to represent them in matters related to God, to offer gifts and sacrifices for sins. He is able to deal gently with those who are ignorant and are going astray, since he himself is subject to weakness. This is why he has to offer sacrifices for

his own sins, as well as for the sins of the people.
(Heb. 5:1–3)

When those in ministry project an image of pristine
perfection, they may be respected and admired, but they
also give the impression that they are far above the
problems and concerns of ordinary people. But when
they admit that they too have real struggles, an amazing
thing happens. Their ministry isn't discredited; it is
empowered.

A few years ago I was at a Zondervan sales conference where Bill Hybels, who is pastor of Willow Creek
Community Church, and Becky Pippert, who is a well-
known evangelist, author, and speaker, were asked to
talk about books they each had written.

Bill spoke first about his new book on marriage,
entitled *Fit To Be Tied*. He began with a confession. He
said that he and his wife, Lynn, are about as opposite as
two people could be. He admitted that under the best of
circumstances they have a difficult marriage, and at
times it is *very* difficult. He told those present that he
didn't claim to have all the answers about marriage but
that he hoped he could share some insights that he and
Lynn had learned as they struggled to make their marriage better.

Next Becky Pippert came to the podium to speak
about her book *Hope Has Its Reasons*. She too began with
a confession, one that stunned the audience. She said,
"Rumors are beginning to circulate about me and my
husband. Because you will be representing my book to
people, I feel that you deserve to hear the truth directly

from me rather than secondhand. My husband and I are separated, and we covet your prayers. You may also have heard gossip about my husband, but I want you to know that the gossip did not originate with me. Now, if you will allow me, I would like to speak to you about God's grace and forgiveness."

During her talk that followed, the room was filled with both silence and the presence of God. I have heard both Becky Pippert and Bill Hybels speak on several occasions, but that day they seemed most human and spoke with a power and conviction that far surpassed anything I had ever heard from them before. In their brokenness, they offered hope and healing to those who, like them, were struggling to be faithful to Jesus Christ.

Please don't think I am saying that we must have bad marriages or go through a separation or divorce in order to have effective ministries. That would be equivalent to Paul's question to the Romans, "Shall we go on sinning so that grace may increase?" (Rom. 6:1). God calls each one of us to live holy lives before him, and he requires spiritual maturity in those who are leaders in the church (1 Tim. 3). But even leaders are not perfect, as Paul himself admitted to the Philippians:

> Not that I have already obtained all this, or have already been made perfect, but I press on to take hold of that for which Christ Jesus took hold of me. Brothers, I do not consider myself yet to have taken hold of it. But one thing I do: Forgetting what is behind and straining toward what is ahead, I press on toward the goal to win the prize for which God

has called me heavenward in Christ Jesus. (Phil. 3:12–14)

My former mother-in-law was a member of Alcoholics Anonymous for nearly twenty years, even though she had not taken a drink in all that time. Yet in spite of her sobriety, whenever she spoke at an AA meeting, she would begin by saying, "My name is Rose, and I'm an alcoholic." According to her, that is standard procedure for anyone in the organization.

How I wish the church could learn that one lesson from AA. Instead of always presenting the Christian life as a before-and-after story—with everything after being sweetness and light—think what would happen if each one of us could say, "My name is Jack [or whatever], and I am a sinner who is being saved by God's grace." I think it would transform our lives and ministries.

PUTTING AWAY CHILDISH WAYS

After all these years, Superman is still my favorite comic-book hero. I have *always* wanted to be faster than a speeding bullet, more powerful than a locomotive, and able to leap tall buildings in a single bound. Like two young kids, my wife and I faithfully watch *Lois & Clark: The New Adventures of Superman* every week. Childhood fantasies die hard!

Not long ago while I was visiting my parents in Dallas I mentioned the cape my mother had made me when I was a child. To my astonishment she said, "I think I still have it here somewhere." She disappeared for a few minutes and then returned with it neatly folded. There it was, just as I had remembered it—the tiny red cape with a yellow **S** hand stitched on the back, and the top corners still wrinkled from tying it around my neck. I hadn't seen the cape in over thirty years, and wonderful memories flooded my mind.

That cape now sits neatly and safely folded in a closet just outside the room where I am working. Occasionally I am still tempted to put it on, especially when I need strength or security. But for now, at least, I think I will leave it where it is. I have found a better way.

NOTES

Chapter 1. I Wish I Were Superman

1. This quote is from *Superman: The Movie* (Warner Bros, 1978).

2. Garrison Keillor, "A Day in the Life of Clarence Bunsen," from the tape *News From Lake Wobegon: Spring* (Minnesota Public Radio, 1993).

3. *Superman: The Movie.*

4. The lump turned out to be harmless, and it was easily removed by surgery.

Chapter 2. God Loves Ninety-Pound Weaklings

1. I eventually joined this second group, and many of its members became my closest and dearest friends. They turned out not to be geeks or nerds at all, but rather students who were highly commited to Jesus Christ and to sharing the gospel on campus.

2. Dr. Seuss, *Yertle the Turtle and Other Stories* (New York: Random House, 1950).

3. Stephen W. Hawking, *A Brief History of Time* (New York: Bantam, 1988), x.

4. *Websters Ninth New Collegiate Dictionary* (Springfield, Mass.: Merriam-Webster, Inc., 1989).

5. C. S. Lewis, *The Weight of Glory and Other Addresses* (New York: Macmillan, 1949), 96–97.

Chapter 3. The Strength of Weakness

1. See Phillip Edgcomb Hughes, "2 Corinthians," *The New International Commentary* (Grand Rapids: Eerdmans, 1962), 442–46.

2. C. S. Lewis, *Mere Christianity* (New York: Macmillian, 1943), 109.

3. Joni Eareckson Tada, "Among Friends," *Moody Monthly* (January 1994), 28.

Chapter 4. God's Wobbly Warriors

1. John Seel, *The Evangelical Forfeit* (Grand Rapids: Baker, 1993), 93.

2. See 2 Corinthians 11:5.

3. Acts of Paul and Thecla 3, as quoted in the *Zondervan Pictorial Encyclopedia of the Bible*, vol. 5, ed. Merrill C. Tenney (Grand Rapids: Zondervan, 1975), 625.

4. "A University of Pittsburgh study of the last decade showed that a tall MBA graduate averages $600 more per year for each extra inch in height. In his 1994 book 'The Truth About Your Height' (Reventropy Associates, San Diego, (619) 576-9283), author Thomas T. Samaras agrees there are more talls in high-level jobs. He says his studies conclude that jobs traditionally biased towards tall people include corporate executives, managers, stockbrokers, television newscasters, consultants and models." Joyce Lain Kennedy, "Want a Better Job? Grow," *Grand Rapids Press* (Tuesday, January 10, 1995).

5. Gordon Fee & Doug Stuart, *How to Read the Bible for All Its Worth: 2nd ed.* (Grand Rapids: Zondervan, 1993), 81.

6. The information and quotes about Harry Moorhouse have been taken from John Pollock, *Moody: The Biography* (Chicago: Moody Press, 1963, 1983), 85–91.

7. Ibid., 89.

8. Ibid., 90.

9. Ibid., 89.

10. Ibid., 91.

Chapter 5. Who Says Bigger Is Better?

1. As quoted by Hank Hanegraaff, *Christianity in Crisis* (Eugene, Ore.: Harvest House, 1993), 202.

2. Ibid., 203.

3. As quoted in *Christianity in Crisis*, 186.

4. Richard Reeves, "Let's Get Motivated," *Time* (May 2, 1994), 66–68. In fairness, I should say that I did not attend Success 1994, so I have no firsthand information on which to evaluate the seminar. But Reeves' article seemed to pinpoint many of the ways in which secular thinking has infected much of Evangelical Christianity, and I *have* had many personal encounters with Christians who embrace this kind of thinking.

5. Ibid., 66.

6. Ibid.

7. Ibid.

8. Of course, we should not make the opposite mistake and think that God is opposed to numbers. After all, Paul tells us that the Lord "wants all men to be saved and to come to a knowledge of the truth" (1 Tim. 2:4). But the size of a crowd does not tell us anything about the spiritual state of people's hearts. So it is quite possible that a small church with highly committed people may be more successful in God's eyes than a large church filled with people who are there for the wrong reasons. I think that Rick Warren, author of the soon to be published book *The Purpose-Driven Church* (Grand Rapids: Zondervan, 1995), strikes the proper balance when he says that bigger is not necessarily better, and smaller is not necessarily better. Better is better!

9. Joseph T. Bayly, *Out of My Mind* (Grand Rapids: Zondervan, 1993), 179–80. The order of some of the material has been rearranged.

10. This quote and the other information on David Brainerd is from Ruth A. Tucker, *From Jerusalem to Irian Jaya* (Grand Rapids: Zondervan, 1983), 90–94.

11. As quoted by Mark Galli, "The Man Who Wouldn't Give Up," *Christian History*, issue 36, vol. XI, no. 4, 11. The other material on Carey is also derived from this article.

12. Ibid., 15.

Chapter 6. The Power of Plainness

1. Rebecca Manley Pippert, *Out of the Saltshaker* (Downers Grove, Ill.: InterVarsity Press, 1979), 15.

2. Pollock, *Moody*, 28.

3. Ibid., 167–68.

4. Ibid., 170–71.

5. Ibid., 160–61.

6. Spurgeon, C. H., *Autobiography: Vol. 1—The Early Years, 1834–1859* (Carlisle, Penn.: Banner of Truth Trust, 1962), 87–88.

7. Ibid., 88.

8. Pollock, *Moody*, 27.

9. Ibid., 27.

10. Woodbridge, John, ed., *More Than Conquerors* (Chicago: Moody, 1992), 50–51.

11. Colson, Charles W., *Born Again* (Grand Rapids: Zondervan, 1976), 114–17.

Chapter 7. So You're a Toe!

1. This statement was made on another occasion rather than at the memorial service, but it is typical of the thoughts of many who were present.

Chapter 8. Lord, Please Use Someone Else!

1. C. H. Spurgeon, *Lectures to My Students* (Grand Rapids: Baker, 1977), 173.

2. Notice that I didn't say "expose our fears." It took me quite a while to realize that the opposite of courage is not fear but cowardice. A person can be trembling with fear and still demonstrate amazing courage.

3. *Dale Carnegie's Scrapbook: A Treasure of the Wisdom of the Ages*, ed. Dorothy Carnegie (Garden City, N.Y.: Dale Carnegie & Associates, 1959), 19.

4. C. S. Lewis, *Prince Caspian* (New York: Collier, 1951), 137. The words "if they follow me" are not part of the original quote, but they are an accurate summary of what Aslan says to Lucy in the following paragraphs.

Chapter 9. It Hurts So Good

1. Owen Anderson, "The Inside Dope on Runner's High," *Runner's World* (August, 1994), 61.

2. Ibid., 62.

3. Bob Buford, *Halftime* (Grand Rapids: Zondervan, 1994), 49.

4. Ibid., 51.

Chapter 10. The Power of Transparency

1. This excerpt is from a story by Garrison Keillor entitled "Pastor Ingqvist's Trip to Orlando" on the audio tape *Gospel Birds and Other Stories of Lake Wobegon* (Minnesota Public Radio, 1985).

2. William D. Hendricks, *Exit Interviews: Revealing Stories of Why People Are Leaving the Church* (Chicago: Moody Press, 1993), 32–33.

3. Ibid., 69.

4. Ibid., 260–61.

5. Henri J. M. Nouwen, *The Wounded Healer: Ministry in Contemporary Society* (Garden City, N.Y.: Image, 1979).